5:2 healthy eating for life

5:2 healthy eating for life

delicious calorie-counted recipes for fast days,
family meals and entertaining

Belinda Berry

photography by Graham Berry & Belinda Berry

About the author

Belinda Berry spent several years catering to rock bands on tour and film crews on location before changing her career for one in software development in the telecommunications industry.

Following early retirement in 2000, she and her husband Graham set off on a cruising adventure on their yacht Oasis, spending time in the Mediterranean, Atlantic and Caribbean seas before returning to Europe and settling in France, where they run Images of France photography holidays.

The food she created for her guests became the subject of her first cookery book "Focus on Flavour - recipes inspired by living in South West France".

To learn more about Images of France photography courses and holidays, please visit www.imagefrance.com

About this book

As a long-time passionate organic gardener, Belinda's love of fresh, seasonal foods shines through in this book of delicious, healthy recipes. She and Graham embarked on following the 5:2 Fast Diet in early 2013 and this has inspired the creation of this, her second cookery book.

Please note that the information given in this book is intended as a general guide to healthy eating and is not to be relied upon as medical advice. A qualified medical practitioner or appropriate professional should be consulted for any specific health problems.

Follow Belinda's 5:2 Healthy Eating for Life blog at www.focusonflavour.com

First edition published December 2013

ISBN-13: 978-1494351533

ISBN-10: 1494351536

Dedication

to

Lexi Sky Rowland Tickner

a life-limited baby with cerebral palsy,
muscular dystrophy and epilepsy.

Some days, even breathing is difficult for this little girl.

To make her life as enjoyable and comfortable as possible,
her parents have become full-time carers
and she has many needs for equipment and support.

A donation to her support fund will be made for every book sold.

http://gogetfunding.com/project/lexi-sky-rowland-tickner

Contents

Introduction

Why 5:2?

As New Year arrived I came to a realisation that I had to do something about the weight that had crept up on me over the years. I was feeling sluggish and shapeless and concerned about the prospect of diabetes and heart disease.

I have tried calorie-restricted diets and various others in the past, but have never managed to find anything that I could stick to or that would give me lasting results. What I needed was something that didn't restrict any particular food groups, but somehow would encourage me to eat more healthily every day, so that I could replace my bad habits with better ones.

Graham saw Dr Michael Mosley talking on TV about 5:2 Intermittent Fasting and was excited by what he heard. Here was a way of eating that could not only help us to lose excess weight, but would also increase the prospect of living longer in better health, reducing our risk of life-shortening disease. I wanted to learn more about the science behind the idea and to understand how to go about it. We ordered "The 5:2 Fast Diet" book and as soon as I had read the first few chapters I was eager to get started.

Without radically changing our lifestyle, we incorporated two low calorie fasting days a week (500 calories for me, 600 for him). The other 5 days we worked on getting our portion sizes under control and cutting back on some of the things that we knew were not helpful to us - bread, alcohol, pastry and chocolate. Nothing had to be excluded completely, but interestingly, the fast days helped by decreasing our appetite and encouraging us to enjoy more salads and fresh foods.

Having learned that it is ok to be hungry, that one can get through the day without eating lunch, one starts to become aware of how often we eat for the wrong reasons. Because we are tired, bored or emotional. Because it is a habit. Because we have cravings. Because it is there.

It became easier for me to stop eating before I was full. I stopped craving sugary and salty snacks. I found that I liked the clean feeling that follows a fast day, so that after a weekend of indulging in a few treats, it feels good to have a day of light eating.

After less than 6 months of following this way of eating, I had lost 14.5 kilos and reached my target weight, with a healthy BMI of 23 (down from 29.45).

I am optimistic that it is not too late to reverse the trend towards diabetes, heart disease, arthritis, high blood pressure, Alzheimer's and whatever other ailments we may have been heading for. The research into Intermittent Fasting shows great promise in these areas, and the anecdotal evidence from thousands of people following the 5:2 way of eating is bearing witness to it.

The recipes in this book are all calorie-counted. During the course of the year I have worked with seasonal ingredients and developed menus that celebrate and feature them. Some recipes are ideal for fast days - others more suited for weekends, dinner parties, summer barbecues or everyday family meals. Whether you are following the 5:2 way of eating or are just looking for some delicious and flavourful recipes to share with family and friends, I hope you will enjoy them.

Bon Appétit!

Seasonal and Local

Living in South West France for the last 10 years, I have become used to the seasonal availability of fresh produce. In the local markets you would never find peaches or tomatoes in February or satsumas in July. So I welcome the arrival of the first spears of asparagus in late March, celebrate the short season of the various soft and tree fruits, mourn the last of the fresh basil and look forward to next year's harvest of strawberries.

We naturally want to eat light, fresh salads in the heat of the summer and hanker after warming, hearty soups and casseroles in the chilly winter months. This goes along with what is seasonally abundant and therefore cheaper. Of course we have the advantage of frozen foods to extend the availability of produce and nowadays we all expect to be able to buy bananas, avocados, root ginger, limes and so on at any time of the year. But it is well worth trying to reduce food miles for the benefit of both the planet and your purse. Whilst local may be ideal, the next best thing is to choose foods that are in season wherever they have been grown. Produce grown outdoors without the need for artificial fertilisers and heat will usually taste better and be cheaper.

My own vegetable and fruit garden is managed organically and by preference I would always choose organically grown produce, but it does often cost more. The interesting thing is that by eating less we have actually cut our food bill quite significantly, so that I can more easily afford to choose organic.

Delicious, Full of Flavour and Satisfying

I've really enjoyed the challenge of finding interesting, flavourful food that is filling but not fattening and getting creative with those few calories. We frequently have a 3-course dinner on our fast days and enjoy every mouthful. When you don't have much on your plate, it is all the more important that what you choose is tasty and satisfying. I use lots of fresh herbs, spices and small amounts of strong flavours to create zingy and delicious meals that leave you with the feeling of having eaten very well indeed, but not at all bloated or over-stuffed.

I often serve soups as a way of gently re-introducing food after a whole day without, they really help to fill you up and are often quick and easy to make, making the most of seasonal vegetables and providing a great platform for introducing new and exciting flavours.

Whilst you don't need to exclude anything in particular long term, in the short term it is worth saying no to French patisserie, buttery pastry, rich creamy sauces and so on, while working on getting to your maintenance weight. Weekends and the occasional night out can still include a couple of glasses of wine and a delicious dessert without making you feel guilty. But don't deny yourself flavour - a good-looking plate of food with fantastic aromas will satisfy the mind as well as the body. The two work together to manage our appetite, so it is worth pleasing the eye and the nose as well as filling the stomach!

Yes there is some willpower required to keep going on a fast day, to wait another 15 minutes before having something to eat, to say no to a cream cake or whatever is your weakness – but the goals of being healthy, looking good, and best of all, feeling good – well those are worth working for, worth a little short-term discomfort. And that's all it is, a little discomfort. You won't be starving.

Healthy Eating for Life

The act of fasting twice a week helps to reduce your stomach size, reduce your appetite and reduce your cravings. It makes you more mindful about what and when you eat and to not mind being a little hungry occasionally. If you combine this with steps towards avoiding junk food, cutting back on snacking and sweetened soft drinks and replacing processed and refined foods with fresh, seasonal, home-made and whole foods wherever you can, then you will be well on the way to a really healthy lifestyle, even if you don't take any more exercise.

Aim for a wide variety of foods, in as natural as state as possible and keep cooking times to a minimum, in order to have a wide range of vitamins, minerals and trace elements in your diet.

Since reaching our target weights, we still continue with 2 fast days a week for the long-term health benefits. To avoid continuing to lose too much weight, I have added back in some of the calorie-dense foods that we love, like nuts, avocados, cheese and bananas. I am a little more generous with oil and tend to choose full fat dairy produce. These measures help us to maintain our weight whilst still eating healthily.

Carbs/Fats/Proteins

Throughout this book, I have included the nutritional information on how many grams of carbohydrates, fats and proteins are in each recipe, for those who wish to keep track. The figures are rounded to the nearest whole unit, per serving.

Carbs

Generally we think of carbohydrates in terms of starchy foods, like potatoes, rice and pasta or sweet foods like sugar and fruits, but there are carbs in grains, vegetables, fruits and dairy products. In general, aim for carbohydrates with a low GI (Glycaemic Index), as these will be more satisfying and will have less impact on your insulin levels. That means using whole grains instead of refined and having an awareness of the natural sugar content of foods, which is what makes them spike your blood sugar levels. The GI of a food can be lowered by combining it with fats, so do

consider using a little butter with your potato.

I try and use unrefined produce as far as practical - stoneground whole wheat flour, brown or wild rice, wholewheat pasta, whole grains, raw sugar and keep refined white products to a minimum.

My recommendation is that portion sizes of starchy carbohydrates should be no bigger than your fist, on any day of the week.

There is no need to avoid carbohydrates altogether though and one of the beauties of 5:2 is that you don't need to exclude any food group and can continue to enjoy fruits and vegetables in abundance.

What you will find is that starchy carbs have lots of calories, so avoiding them on a fast day allows you to get a larger and more satisfying meal. Cauliflower is an amazing low-calorie substitute for starchy carbs like potatoes, rice and pizza bases on fast days.

Do watch out for fruit juice and smoothies, which lots of people think of as 'healthy' foods. In fact, because you are eating several pieces of fruit all in one go without the fibre, juices and smoothies can be very high in fructose, which can result not only in putting on weight, but in spiking blood sugar and lead to cravings for more carbohydrates.

Proteins

According to the advice given to Dr Mosley by Prof Valter Longo, for longevity we should be keeping the amount of protein that we eat to under 0.85g per kilo of body weight and to use more plant based proteins. For many in the western world that means cutting back on meat, fish and eggs and instead looking at nuts, seeds or legumes (beans or pulses) as sources of protein. I tend to keep our portion sizes of protein much smaller now, and bulk up our meals with plenty of fresh vegetables and fruit.

On fast days it is important to have a good amount of protein, which is satiating and also important to help keep our brains and our friendly gut bacteria happy.

Fats

I'm no longer afraid of good fats - once tagged as the culprits for rising rates of heart disease and diabetes - and rather see sugar as one of the major sources of inflammation in the body. So I use real butter, cream and cold-pressed oils which add flavour and create a feeling of satisfaction. There is still a place for skimmed milk dairy products, especially on fast days, when calories are precious, but I do try to avoid packaged products that are labelled as low-fat, as so often they contain sweeteners, fillers and other additives to compensate for the absence of fat.

Calorie Counting and Tracking

Calorie counts are at best a close estimate of the energy value of a given food. The method of cooking or processing, the ripeness or age of the food and various other factors may all have an influence - and then there is the added variation of your own metabolism. We vary so much in how efficiently we burn those calories.

I have used various sources to get the nutrient values for my recipes - MyFitnessPal, Calorie Count and the RecipeCard plugin for my Wordpress blog - and I usually cross check with the USDA database. Google is amazingly handy if you want to quickly check the calorie count for a specific ingredient – just type in 'calories in xxxx' and it pops up a useful table, with drop-down options for varieties of the ingredient and serving sizes, based on the USDA figures. If you Google for 'nutrition in xxxx' you will get a complete breakdown of carbs, protein and fats as well as calories. Most packaged foods now have the calorie and nutritional values on the packet too.

The calorie counts I have given, rounded up to the nearest 5, will give you a good idea of what you can include on a Fast Day to add up to 500 or 600 calories – but those figures too are just a guide. The suggestion is that you should be eating a quarter of your normal intake on a fast day – but for me that would be well under 500, which is a bit mean - and for someone very active it could mean closer to 800. So don't stress about a few calories over or under. The objective is to make your fast days do-able, but to be making a significant calorie restriction compared to a normal day.

By the way, calories should really be called kilocalories, which is why you will find them as kcals throughout the recipes.

Portion Sizes

I find that many recipes create far more than we can actually eat and when you calorie count them it helps to understand why so many people are overweight - basically we eat too much! Now I serve less and we no longer feel that we need to finish everything on our plates or in the serving dish.

Our Total Daily Energy Expenditure (TDEE) is the amount of calories that we need in a day to stay the same weight. This figure is calculated based on your age, sex, height, weight and activity level, so whilst the average may be 2000 for a woman and 2500 for a man, in reality there is a huge variation for individuals. My own TDEE without accounting for any extra exercise is about 1400, whereas my husband needs 2200.

So portion sizes are going to be different for different people. When a recipe serves 2 that will usually be enough for one large and one smaller portion. I have sometimes given different portion sizes for 500 or 600-calorie meals on fast days. I have also shown the calories for each ingredient so that you can easily increase or decrease the amounts you use.

Sweet Nothings…

I've found that there seems to be a complete obsession with adding sweetness to things, even in so-called healthy recipes.

Case in point: For a Sunday lunch, I cooked braised red cabbage. The recipe called for a tablespoon of brown sugar – but it didn't need it, a drop of aged balsamic brought out the sweetness. I made a parsnip dish, the recipe called for a tablespoon of honey - parsnips are naturally sweet, they don't need any extra…. I made a pear dessert, the recipe called for a tablespoon of honey per person - again, pears already have natural sugars, so I added a just teaspoonful between us, which was plenty. If I had followed the recipes without thinking, we each would have consumed an extra two tablespoonfuls of sweetness each. I don't think the food would have tasted any better for it…

If you can stop having sweeteners in drinks like tea and coffee, then it becomes possible to appreciate the natural sweetness of fruits and vegetables and the amount of sugar that you use can be dramatically reduced.

Herb teas, mineral water with a slice of lemon, lemon juice with ginger and hot water, rooibos tea, sassy water – these are refreshing and make good alternatives. If you usually add sugar to tea or coffee, try to avoid them on a fast day as even artificial sweeteners can make your body respond as if it was having sugar. The chemicals and processing methods, even of the so-called natural sweeteners like agave syrup, are probably best avoided when considering our long-term health.

Try and make a fast day a day of sweet nothings.

How the Book is Organised

The recipes are grouped in to chapters according to the types of dish (Soups, Desserts etc.) or the main ingredient (Eggs, Fish, Meat etc.).

I have used British terminology and metric measurements in general. Sometimes I use French names for things as I have got accustomed to them and probably don't realise that they are called something else, so apologies for that!

I have included a glossary of ingredients towards the end of the book, which should help to answer any questions about what things are and what can be substituted in case of difficulty and I have also noted foods that are known by different names in North America and Australia.

Then there are conversion tables between metric and imperial measurements and temperatures.

Please note that I cook with a fan-assisted oven, so those are the temperatures I have used throughout and the timings are related to my own experience. Be aware that ovens vary, so be cautious with temperatures and timings until you have an idea as to whether your oven behaves similarly to mine!

For those who like to use meal plans, I have included some examples and created some special themed menus to encourage exploration of different food styles.

I hope you will find some useful and inspiring ideas here to help you to keep going with 5:2 in the long term, along with us.

If you are not following 5:2 you will still find plenty of light and delicious recipes here, suitable for everyday family meals and entertaining.

This is a recipe book - not a book about Intermittent Fasting - so if you would like to know more about 5:2, please read "The Fast Diet" by Dr Michael Mosley and Mimi Spencer. I can't recommend it highly enough!

"*To eat is a necessity,*

but to eat intelligently is an art."

~ François de La Rochefoucauld

Soup is a favourite for Fast Days – quickly taking the edge off your appetite and helping to make the process of eating a slower affair altogether.

I love to showcase vegetables with simple soups using only a few ingredients.

A hand (stick) blender is invaluable as it means you can whizz up the soup and create the texture you want without creating additional washing up.

I sometimes make my own chicken stock (when poaching chicken, or with the leftover carcass from a roast), which I then chill so that the fat can be separated off, but I find that Swiss vegetable bouillon powder works very well as an easy way to make a stock for soup.

Serving size is 2 ladles per person or about 200 – 250ml. Bear this in mind when scaling recipes up or down and make sure that you add enough liquid.

Mushroom and Celery Soup

A combination of ingredients that work surprisingly well together, to make a very low calorie, yet substantial soup, that combines interesting flavours and textures. Declared "very satisfying and kind of meaty". Perfect for a 5:2 Fast Day.

Serves 4

- 250g mushrooms, chopped 55 kcals
- 4 stalks of celery, chopped 35 kcals
- 3 cloves garlic, finely chopped 13 kcals
- 1 litre stock, made with 2tsp of bouillon powder 24 kcals
- 1 tsp Worcestershire sauce 5 kcals
- 1 tsp grated nutmeg 12 kcals
- Sea salt and freshly ground black pepper
- Celery leaves, finely chopped

Put the mushrooms, garlic and celery in a saucepan with about 100ml of stock.

Cover and cook over a low heat until the celery is soft, about 30 - 40 minutes.

Add half of the remaining stock and whizz with a blender. Pour in the rest of the stock together with the Worcestershire sauce and nutmeg. Bring to the boil, then check the seasoning.

Serve garnished with celery leaves.

Per serving: kcals 36
Carbs 6g Fat 1g Protein 3g

Carrot and Coriander Soup

Celebrate carrots with this lovely simple soup. Ok, this is a favourite to buy ready made, but it is easy to make yourself and you get to choose the carrots that go into it, so go for organically grown carrots for bags of flavour.

Serves 4

- 500g carrots, scrubbed or peeled and sliced 175 kcals
- 1 onion, peeled and chopped 46 kcals
- 1.2 litres stock made with 2 tsp Marigold bouillon powder 24 kcals
- 1 tbsp olive oil 120 kcals
- 3 tsp coriander seeds 15 kcals
- 1 bunch of fresh coriander leaves, finely chopped 6 kcals
- Sea salt and freshly ground black pepper

Toast the coriander seeds lightly in a dry frying pan, then grind coarsely.

Heat the oil in a heavy saucepan and add the onions and carrots. Cook gently for a few minutes until starting to soften, but not colour. Add most of the coriander seeds and mix well, reserving a few for garnish. Season with pepper and salt (if your stock isn't already salty). Add the stock, bring to the boil and simmer for 10 minutes or until the carrots are tender. Whizz with a stick blender then add most of the coriander leaves. Serve garnished with chopped coriander leaves and a sprinkling of seeds. On a non-fast day you could add a swirl of crème fraîche when serving.

Per serving: kcals 97
Carbs 15g Fat 5g Protein 2g

Hot and Sour Soup (Tom Yum)

A deliciously light and spicy soup that can be made with prawns, chicken, mushrooms or tofu.

I had forgotten how great this soup tastes! Spicy, slightly sweet, sour, bitter, salty – it has that umami savoury satisfaction factor. Adapted From *"The Taste Of Thailand"* By Vatcharin Bhumichitr.

Serves 4

1 litre chicken or vegetable stock 24 kcals

1 tsp Thai red curry paste 20 kcals

1 tbsp Thai fish sauce (Nam Pla) 4 kcals

1/2 lemon or lime, juice only 6 kcals

2 lime leaves, finely sliced 3 kcals

5cm of lemon grass stalk, finely sliced 15 kcals

100g mushrooms (fresh chestnut or button, or canned straw mushrooms), sliced 22 kcals

1 spring onion, sliced 5 kcals

A few coriander leaves

A few birds eye chillies 3 kcals

200g of peeled and deveined prawns 167 kcals

- OR 175g shredded chicken 170 kcals

- OR 100g cubed tofu 164 kcals

Heat the stock in a saucepan and add the curry paste, fish sauce, lime leaves, lemon grass, lemon juice and chillies.

Taste and add more curry paste if necessary.

Bring to the boil and simmer for a couple of minutes.

Add the mushrooms, the prawns or chicken and the spring onion and simmer for a further 2-3 minutes until the prawns are cooked or the chicken heated through.

Serve decorated with coriander leaves and a couple of bird's eye chillies.

The fish sauce is a key part of the flavour combination, but for strict vegetarians you could substitute soy sauce and a little sugar and use tofu or mushrooms as the main ingredient. Lime leaves and lemongrass can be used straight from the freezer.

Per serving: kcals 76
Carbs 6g Fat 1g Protein 12g

Simple Vegetable Soup

Quick and easy, using frozen prepared vegetables for soup (e.g. carrot, courgette, cauliflower, turnip, green beans, potato) and bouillon powder – this is a really useful standby recipe for a fast day, which can be varied by using different combinations of vegetables and altering the texture from a clear broth to a completely smooth purée. I usually go for somewhere in between, leaving some chunky pieces of vegetables, as shown.

Serves 1

100g frozen or fresh chopped mixed vegetables 52 kcals

1 tsp Marigold bouillon powder 12 kcals

250ml water

Put the vegetables in a saucepan and add the water and bouillon powder. Bring to the boil then simmer for 10 minutes.

Whizz with a stick blender to desired texture, or leave as a broth with veggie pieces.

Per serving: kcals 64
Carbs 13g Fat 1g Protein 3g

Simple Vegetable Soup - Thai Style

A variation of **Simple Vegetable Soup** using a stir-fry mix which contains vegetables like mange tout, baby corn, mushrooms, bean shoots, sweet pepper and bamboo shoots. Adding some Thai style red curry paste and a little coconut milk completes the transformation.

Serves 1

100g frozen vegetables for stir-fries 58 kcals

1 tsp marigold bouillon 12 kcals

1/2 tsp Thai red curry paste 2 kcals

1 tbsp low-fat coconut milk 35 kcals

Chopped coriander leaves, to garnish

Put the vegetables in a saucepan along with the water, bouillon powder and curry paste. Simmer 10 minutes. Just before serving, stir in the coconut milk.

Garnish with chopped coriander leaves.

Per serving: kcals 107
Carbs 16g Fat 5g Protein 4g

Watercress Soup

Watercress is rich in vitamins A and C, calcium, iron and folic acid. A big bunch makes an easy and delicious soup in less than 30 minutes. Just the thing to break your fast with. I use potato flakes as it saves a lot of time, but if you have leftover cooked potato you could use that, to give the soup a little more body.

Serves 4

1 large bunch (450g) watercress 50 kcals

1 medium onion, chopped 46 kcals

10g unsalted butter 74 kcals

1 litre of vegetable stock, made with 10g Marigold bouillon powder 24 kcals

10g potato flakes 35 kcals

A grating of nutmeg 3 kcals

Sea salt and freshly ground black pepper

Discard any really coarse stalks from the watercress, as they can be too peppery.

Wash, drain and chop the remainder of the bunch, reserving a few tips for decoration.

Heat the butter in a large pan and gently sauté the onions, stirring from time to time, until softened but not coloured.

Add the chopped watercress, stock, nutmeg and the potato flakes, then simmer gently for about 10 minutes. Blend until smooth.

Serve with a garnish of watercress leaves, or a swirl of crème fraîche.

Add 35 calories for a slice of crispbread and 10 calories for a teaspoonful of crème fraîche

Per serving: kcals 60
Carbs 7g Fat 3g Protein 3g

Italian Vegetable Soup

A little pesto and a sprinkle of Parmesan bring a taste of Italy to a straightforward vegetable soup. There is lots of scope for varying the vegetables according to the season.

Serves 2

½ tbsp olive oil 60 kcals

½ large onion, chopped 30 kcals

1 clove garlic, finely chopped 4 kcals

1 stalk celery, chopped 10 kcals

¼ cauliflower florets (150g) 38 kcals

1 medium carrot, chopped 26 kcals

¼ sweet red bell pepper, chopped 10 kcals

1 tbsp parsley, finely chopped 2 kcals

500ml chicken or vegetable stock 12 kcals

1 tsp pesto 22 kcals

Sea salt and freshly ground black pepper

To serve:

A few basil leaves, roughly torn

10g freshly grated Parmesan cheese 32 kcals

Heat oil in large pan and gently sauté the onions and garlic for about 5 minutes, until a little softened. Then add the celery, carrot and red pepper and cook gently for a further 10 minutes, adding a little water if necessary to prevent them sticking. Add the cauliflower, parsley and stock, bring to the boil and simmer for 10 to 12 minutes until the cauliflower is tender.

Add the pesto and adjust the seasoning to taste.

Serve in warmed bowls with some basil leaves and a sprinkle of Parmesan.

Per serving: kcals 124
Carbs 14g Fat 6g Protein 5g

Spring Minestrone

For me, broad beans and asparagus are star ingredients when they are in season. Just a spoonful of crème fraîche and some basil oil gives this soup some extra va va voom and transforms a simple vegetable soup into something luxurious.

Serves 4

> **1 tbsp olive oil 120 kcals**
>
> **1 leek, chopped quite small 56 kcals**
>
> **1 litre vegetable stock, made with 2 tsp vegetable bouillon 24 kcals**
>
> **1 clove garlic, finely chopped 4 kcals**
>
> **250g green asparagus, trimmed, cut in 1cm slices 52 kcals**
>
> **250g shelled broad beans 212 kcals**
>
> **1 tbsp half fat crème fraîche 24 kcals**
>
> **1 tsp basil oil (or pesto) 16 kcals**

To garnish

> **25g freshly grated Parmesan 80 kcals**

Heat olive oil and cook leek gently until soft.

Add stock and garlic and simmer for 10 minutes.

Add remaining vegetables and simmer for a further 5 - 7 minutes.

Stir in crème fraîche and pesto.

Serve sprinkled with Parmesan.

Per serving: kcals 150
Carbs 14g Fat 7g protein 10g

Bargeman's Tomato Soup

I came across this recipe in a book about cooking on a canal barge by Kate Ratliffe *"A Culinary Journey in Gascony"*. It makes a wonderful summery soup using loads of fresh tomatoes, but I thought it would be perfect for a fast day even in winter using tinned, bottled or frozen tomatoes. Adding an egg just before the end of cooking increases the protein content and gives added interest. I would serve this over some toasted bread rubbed with garlic for a non-fast day.

Serves 2

> **1 can (425g) of chopped tomatoes, or 500g fresh tomatoes, peeled and crushed 74 kcals**
>
> **1 onion, roughly chopped 46 kcals**
>
> **4 cloves of garlic, crushed 13 kcals**
>
> **500ml water**
>
> **Sea salt and freshly ground black pepper**
>
> **1 large egg 70 kcals**
>
> **A couple of sprigs of fresh thyme, leaves stripped from the stalk (or a tsp of dried thyme) or fresh basil, chopped**

Put the tomatoes, onion and garlic into a pan along with the water and season well.

Bring to the boil, then simmer for 15 minutes.

Bring back to a boil, beat the egg lightly and stir into the soup.

Check and adjust the seasoning to taste.

Remove from the heat and stir in the herbs.

Per serving: kcals 110
Carbs 13g Fat 3g Protein 6g

Moroccan Cauliflower Soup

Cauliflower soup has long been a favourite of mine, since I first came across it as Potage Dubarry - a pale, creamy soup. Cauliflower has an amazing affinity with spicy flavours and works wonderfully well with the heat and aroma of the Maghreb (North West Africa).

Serves 6

> **1 large cauliflower, cut into florets 210 kcals**
>
> **1 tbsp olive oil 120 kcals**
>
> **½ tsp ground cinnamon 3 kcals**
>
> **1 tsp ground cumin 8 kcals**
>
> **1 tsp ground coriander 5 kcals**
>
> **1 tbsp harissa paste 10 kcals**
>
> **2 litres chicken or vegetable stock, made with stock cube or bouillon powder 24 kcals**
>
> **30g toasted flaked almonds 140 kcals**

For serving

> **1 tsp harissa paste 3 kcals**
>
> **1 tsp lemon juice 1 kcal**

Heat the oil in a large pan and gently fry the spices together with the harissa paste, for a couple of minutes. Add the cauliflower and stock and most of the almonds, reserving some for decoration.

Bring to the boil, cover and lower heat to simmer for 20 minutes, until the cauliflower is tender. Whizz with a hand blender until smooth.

To serve, mix harissa paste with lemon juice to make a swirl for decorating and sprinkle flaked almonds over the top.

Per serving: kcals 87
Carbs 10g Fat 5g Protein 4g

Caribbean Butternut Squash Soup

This recipe works equally well with any kind of winter squash. If you blend it until smooth it is creamy and luxurious, or if you leave it slightly chunky it seems wholesome and earthy. This is based on a recipe from *"A Carriacou Cookbook"* by Rosamond Cameron.

Serves 4

> **10g unsalted butter 70 kcals**
>
> **1 onion, chopped 46 kcals**
>
> **1 leek, chopped 54 kcals**
>
> **1 clove garlic, finely chopped 4 kcals**
>
> **2.5cm knob of root ginger, finely chopped 10 kcals**
>
> **500g butternut or other winter squash 210 kcals**
>
> **1 litre chicken or vegetable 24 kcals**
>
> **1 – 2 tsp hot curry powder 25 kcals**
>
> **½ tsp ground ginger 3 kcals**
>
> **½ tsp ground nutmeg 6 kcals**
>
> **Sea salt and freshly ground black pepper**

To serve:

> **1 tbsp chopped coriander or parsley 1 kcal**
>
> **1 tbsp half fat fromage blanc or crème fraîche 25 kcals**

Melt the butter in a large pan. Add the onion, garlic and ginger and cook for 1 minute without browning. Add the spices, stir then add chopped leek, squash and stock. Bring to the boil, stir and simmer for 20 to 30 minutes until squash is soft. Add seasoning to taste.

Serve sprinkled with chopped herbs and a swirl of cream.

Per serving: kcals 118
Carbs 23g Fat 3g Protein 2g

Tuscan Zucchini Soup

This is a summery and delicious soup that makes a good light lunch or first course. Ideal if you have a glut of courgettes, or some that are a bit on the large side. You can use any shape of courgettes or soft-skinned summer squash. This soup freezes well. Based on a recipe by Annabel Langbein.

Serves 6

> 1kg courgettes (zucchini), diced 160 kcals
> 1 tbsp olive oil 120 kcals
> 4 cloves garlic, finely chopped 17 kcals
> A handful of basil leaves
> 10g (2 tsp) Marigold bouillon powder 24 kcals
> 1.2 litres water
> Sea salt to taste and freshly ground black pepper
> 1 tbsp chopped parsley 1 kcal
> 50g Parmesan cheese, finely grated 160 kcals

Heat the olive oil in a large heavy saucepan.

Add the courgettes, garlic, basil and black pepper. Cover and cook over a low heat for about 10 minutes, until the vegetables are softened.

Set aside a couple of tablespoonfuls of the courgettes for garnish.

Make the stock with boiling water and bouillon powder. Add to the pan and simmer gently for a further 10 minutes. When the courgettes are soft, whizz to a purée with a stick blender.

Taste and adjust seasoning. Stir in parsley and most of the grated Parmesan.

Serve with a little grated Parmesan on top and some pieces of courgette.

Per serving: kcals 89
Carbs 8g Fat 5g Protein 5g

Add another 70 calories for 3 grissini breadsticks.

Recipes often use a lot of oil for sautéing the vegetables, which can add unnecessary extra calories.

Really you just need enough to stop the vegetables from sticking in the first instance and to give a little flavour.

You can use a spray or a silicone brush to coat the surface of the pan without adding more than really necessary, and you can always add a little water to stop the vegetables from sticking to the pan.

Spicy Chickpea and Spinach Soup

Here's a hearty and delicious soup for when you want something more substantial - an ideal winter warmer. I used sunflower oil for sautéing the onions, but I am sure that coconut oil would be great for this. You can vary the green vegetables according to what's available. For a non-fast day a swirl of coconut cream on top and some slivers of toasted coconut would be lovely.

Serves 4

1/2 tbsp sunflower oil 60 kcals

1 onion, chopped 44 kcals

1 clove garlic, chopped 4 kcals

2.5 cm root ginger, finely grated 9 kcals

1/2 fresh green chilli, finely chopped 4 kcals

1 litre vegetable stock 24 kcals

2 large carrots, chopped 58 kcals

400g can of chickpeas, drained 339 kcals

150g spinach leaves, washed and shredded 35 kcals

For the garam masala

1 tsp cumin seeds 8 kcals

1 tsp coriander seeds 5 kcals

1/2 tsp turmeric 4 kcals

1/2 tsp black pepper 3 kcals

1/2 tsp cayenne powder 3 kcals

1/2 tsp ground cinnamon 3 kcals

Heat the oil in heavy pan over low-medium heat and sauté the onion, garlic, ginger and chilli for a few minutes, until the onion starts to become translucent and soft.

Add the garam masala and cook for another couple of minutes, until the spices are fragrant - add a splash of water if necessary to stop them burning.

Add the stock and carrots, bring to the boil and then lower the heat and simmer for 10 minutes or so until the carrots are tender.

Add the chickpeas and then whizz a little with a stick blender, making sure to leave some nice chunky bits.

Add the spinach and cook for a few more minutes until the spinach is wilted.

Serve in warmed bowls.

Per serving: kcals 150
Carbs 23g Fat 4g Protein 7g

Whilst we may have less in the way of cravings for sugary and salty snacks these days, it is good to have something to nibble on when you have a glass of wine or sparkling water with friends before a meal, so in this section there are recipes for some that we enjoy sharing.

Other simple ideas for healthy bites include: -

- air popped corn
- nuts - dry toasted then tossed in butter and herbs or soya sauce
- crisp radishes
- fine slices of air dried ham or cured sausage
- slivers of cheese with a little quince jelly on top
- olives tossed in herbs and garlic
- marinated anchovies
- cherry tomatoes tossed in herbs

Nachos

This is the sort of thing that we might have as a treat at the weekend, especially if we are having a Mexican themed main course, like **Turkey, Red Bean and Chocolate Chilli** (page 116), or **Enchiladas** (page 118). Tortilla corn chips with jalapeno, salsa and grated cheese, heated in the oven until the cheese melts. I try to keep some Red Leicester cheese in the freezer to use with this - it can be grated whilst still frozen. US recipes usually suggest Monterey Jack or Cheddar. If you can't get hold of jalapeno slices, then look for a jar of green chillies - here in France I can usually find Guindillas from Spain.

Serves 2

> **100g tortilla corn chips 218 kcals**
> **1 tbsp sliced pickled jalapenos 2 kcals**
> **2 tbsp medium hot salsa 8 kcals**
> **50g Red Leicester cheese 200 kcals**

Preheat the oven to 160C.

Spread the tortilla chips over a non-stick baking sheet, or one covered with a silicone liner.

Distribute the jalapeno slices and salsa over the chips, then sprinkle with cheese.

Heat in the oven until the cheese has melted.

Per serving: kcals 214
Carbs 24g Fat 10g Protein 9g

Guacamole ~ Avocado Dip

Classic avocado dip which can also be served as a tasty addition to chilli, tacos or tortillas. Avocados are full of good fats, so this a little high in calories, but it is very delicious and nutritious.

Serves 2

> **1 small avocado 250 kcals**
> **1 lemon, juice only 12 kcals**
> **1 tbsp coriander leaves, chopped 5 kcals**
> **1 clove garlic, crushed 4 kcals**
> **1/2 tsp sea salt flakes**
> **Freshly ground black pepper**

Mash the garlic with the salt and coriander leaves, ideally in a pestle and mortar.

Add the lemon juice.

Cut the avocado in half and scoop out the flesh with a spoon, then mash to a fairly smooth texture.

Mix all together and season with pepper.

Optional: To vary this, you can add a skinned chopped tomato, or a spoonful of salsa.

Per serving: kcals 134
Carbs 5g Fat 12g Protein 2g

Serve with crudités or corn chips, or as an accompaniment to **Turkey, Red Bean and Chocolate Chilli** (page 116), or **Enchiladas** (page 118)

Light Hummus ~ Chick Pea Dip with Crudités

I've been making hummus since I was a teenager, when my sister showed me how simple it was to do. Usually I would be more generous with the tahini paste and olive oil, but this worked out well for a fast day and neither of us noticed anything missing. I love the sesame flavour that Tahini adds, which sets apart home-made from so many of the shop bought ones, so don't be tempted to cut it back any further.

Serves 8

> 1 can of chickpeas, drained (265g drained weight) 337 kcals
>
> 25g (about 2 level tbsp) Tahini 160 kcals
>
> Juice of 1 lemon 12 kcals
>
> 1 clove of garlic, crushed 4 kcals
>
> Cold water
>
> Sea salt and freshly ground black pepper
>
> 1/2 tsp cayenne pepper 3 kcals

To garnish:

> 1/2 tsp of extra virgin olive oil 20 kcals
>
> Finely chopped mint or coriander
>
> A pinch of paprika or cayenne

For the crudités:

> 400g celery, cleaned and trimmed 64 kcals
>
> 200g carrot, peeled 80 kcals
>
> 120g radish, washed and trimmed16 kcals
>
> 200g cucumber 32 kcals
>
> 200g fennel, trimmed 64 kcals

Put the chick peas, lemon juice and garlic into a blender and process until almost smooth, adding water as necessary to keep the blender going and to get the consistency the way you like it – firm is good for scooping up with crudités on a fast day, or make it slightly more sloppy for a normal day when you can dip toasted pita bread into it!

Mix in the cayenne pepper and season to taste.

I rarely use salt when cooking these days, but on a fast day it feels like I need a bit to help with hydration.

This amount makes 8 fast day sized helpings of 50grams (approx. 2 tbsp).

Serve in individual dishes (to avoid fighting!) and sprinkle with a little cayenne pepper and a tiny drizzle of olive oil (remembering that 1 tsp of olive oil = 40 kcals....) and some finely chopped mint or coriander.

Cut the vegetables into strips of a suitable size for dipping and serve with the humus.

Per serving: kcals 99
Carbs 14g Fat 3g Protein 4g

For a non-fast day, you could serve with pita bread or tortilla chips.

This is lovely to serve as part of a Greek style menu, with **Lemony Lamb Skewers** (page 106) and **Greek Salad with Feta and Olives** (page 52).

Ingredients for Baba Ganoush ~ Aubergine Dip

Baba Ganoush ~ Aubergine Dip

A tasty dip to serve with any kind of bread, crackers or crudités. You could make it dairy-free by leaving out the yoghurt, though it does help to make it more creamy in texture.

Serves 6

> 1kg aubergine 244 kcals
> 60ml plain yoghurt 24 kcals
> 2 tbsp lemon juice 8 kcals
> 1 clove garlic, crushed 4 kcals
> 60ml Tahini paste 364
> 2 tsp cumin seeds, toasted and ground 16 kcals
> A handful of fresh coriander, chopped 4 kcals
> Sea salt and black pepper

Preheat oven to 180°C (fan).

Toast the cumin seeds in a dry frying pan until lightly coloured and fragrant. Crush in a pestle and mortar. Pierce the aubergine and bake in the oven, uncovered, until soft, about 1 hour.

Cool, then scrape the flesh out with a spoon and add to a blender together with the yoghurt, lemon juice, garlic, Tahini and most of the cumin.

Blend until smooth. Season to taste with salt and freshly ground black pepper.

Garnish with chopped coriander and sprinkle with the remaining crushed seeds.

Per serving: kcals 112
Carbs 13g Fat 6g Protein 4g

Serve with **Maneesh ~ Seedy Flatbread** (page 130 or **Wholewheat Pita** (page 128).

Goats Cheese and Sundried Tomato Aumônières

A very simple and delicious appetiser or canapé. Aumônières are little purses, which would have been used for giving donations to the poor. Your guests will be very pleased with these little gifts!

Makes 6

> 2 sheets of filo pastry 164 kcals
> 1 tsp olive oil 40 kcals
> 28g of soft goats cheese 75 kcals
> 4 sundried tomatoes in oil, drained and finely chopped 15 kcals
> 1 clove garlic, crushed 4 kcals
> 2 tsp finely chopped fresh or 1/2 tsp dried herbs 4 kcals

Preheat oven to 200°C (fan).

Mash the cheese together with the tomatoes, garlic and herbs.

Brush half of one sheet of pastry very lightly with oil, then fold over to transfer it to the other half. Open out again and lay the second sheet on top. Cut into six squares.

Lay a spoonful of the cheese mix in the centre of each square and draw the corners together and gather in the sides, twisting gently to form a purse shape. Place on a non-stick baking sheet and brush very lightly with oil. Bake for about 10 minutes until golden.

Per serving (1): kcals 50
Carbs 6g fat 2g Protein 2g

See the **Pastry** section (page 63) for more ideas on how to use Filo pastry.

"Things on toast" as my mother would have said. You may also think of the Italian bruschetta - slices of toast rubbed with olive oil, or pintxos from the Basque region of Spain, which are small snacks skewered to a piece of bread.

I like to use my own home-made wholewheat bread, but really these will work on whichever type of bread you prefer, such as slices of ciabatta, pain de campagne or baguette.

I don't usually spread any butter on, though sometimes a light brush with olive oil is nice. You can rub the toasted surface with a peeled clove of garlic to add extra flavour.

Sardines on Toast with Avocado Salad

I like the sardines that are canned in olive oil with lemon.

If you don't mind the bones, they are good for your calcium intake.

Serves 2

> **1 can sardines in lemon and olive oil, drained and trimmed 192 kcals**
>
> **2 slices wholewheat bread, toasted 150 kcals**
>
> **1 cup rocket (arugula) leaves 6 kcals**
>
> **2 radishes, finely sliced 2 kcals**
>
> **1/2 carrot, grated 12 kcals**
>
> **1/2 avocado 196 kcals**
>
> **1 tbsp Balsamic and Walnut Vinaigrette (page 124) 26 kcals**

To garnish
> **2 wedges lemon**
>
> **A few baby salad leaves and chopped chives**

Arrange the sardines on the toast.

Scatter with baby salad leaves and serve with a salad composed of rocket, grated carrot, radish and avocado.

Drizzle the dressing over the top of the salad and serve with a wedge of lemon to squeeze over the sardines.

Per serving: kcals 298
Carbs 19g Fat 20g Protein 16g

Goats Cheese and Broad Bean Tartines

I adore broad beans, especially when you can get them young and small, when they don't need peeling. If they are large, I do take the trouble to slip them out of their skins - a slightly tedious task but well worth the effort. I have found doing this has converted people who thought they didn't like broad beans.... You can also buy them frozen, ready peeled. Inspired by Alain Ducasse from his book *"Nature"*.

Serves 1

> **1 slice wholewheat bread 75 kcals**
>
> **1 clove garlic, peeled 4 kcals**
>
> **1 tsp extra virgin olive oil 40 kcals**
>
> **28g soft goat's cheese (one Cabécou) 90 kcals**
>
> **100g baby broad beans, peeled 85 kcals**
>
> **3 radishes, finely sliced 15 kcals**
>
> **1 large spring onion finely sliced 8 kcals**
>
> **Sea salt and freshly ground black pepper**

Cook the broad beans in a small pan of boiling water for about 3 minutes until tender, then drain.

If you have larger beans, cook them for about 5 minutes, drain and leave until cool enough to handle, then slip out of their skins.

Make the toast, rub some garlic over the surface and brush with a little olive oil.

Spread the cheese on top and pile with beans and spring onions.

Top with the radish slices and garnish with salt and pepper.

Per serving: kcals 317
Carbs 30g Fat 15g Protein 16g

Mushrooms on Toast with Grilled Bacon

I do enjoy bacon and there is no reason not to have it occasionally, even if you are trying to lose or maintain your weight. If you choose a nice lean cut of back bacon it is not high in calories and it certainly packs a punch of flavour. Mushrooms are wonderfully low in calories, so you can be as generous as you like with them, but they do absorb oil rather easily. The trick is to add a splash of water while they are cooking, if they seem to be too dry.

Serves 1

1 slice wholewheat toast 75 kcals

1 rasher unsmoked back bacon 53 kcals

1.5 tsp olive oil 60 kcals

1/2 cup mushrooms, cleaned and sliced 11 kcals

1/2 tbsp flat leaf parsley, finely chopped

1 cup mixed salad - lettuce, rocket, tomato, cucumber, radish 13 kcals

1/2 tbsp Balsamic and Walnut Vinaigrette (page 124) 13 kcals

Grill the bacon to your liking.

Heat the olive oil in a non-stick frying pan and add the mushrooms. Stir-fry gently until they soften and look glossy, adding a splash of water if needed. Meanwhile toast the bread.

Add the parsley to the mushrooms, then pile onto the toast and top with the bacon. Serve with a mixed salad, drizzled with the dressing.

Per serving: kcals 225
Carbs 20g Fat 12g Protein 6g

Goat's Cheese Toasts with Baked Beetroot and Spiced Walnuts

"Ooh that was lovely, what was it?" "Beetroot" "Oh, I never liked beetroot…"

I used to make this recipe with fresh baby beetroot, which is good. But this time I made it with packaged pre-cooked organic beetroot. The baking made them caramelised and appealing enough to convert a hardened beetroot-disliker. Combined with the melted goats cheese, rocket, drizzled with a dark balsamic and walnut dressing, and finished off with slightly sweet and spicy walnuts, this is a great marriage of flavours. Makes a great starter for a dinner party, but could equally be a light lunch or supper dish.

If you wish to avoid bread, then make a bigger pile of salad as the base for the goat's cheese.

Based on a recipe by Bill Granger.

Serves 2

> 1 tsp honey 20 kcals
> 1/2 tsp ground cinnamon 3 kcals
> 30g walnut halves or pieces 186 kcals
> 200g cooked beetroot, cut into baby beetroot size chunks 88 kcals
> 2 tsp olive oil 80 kcals
> Sea salt and freshly ground black pepper
> 1 slice wholewheat bread 75 kcals

> 2 Cabecou goats cheese (or 56g of any soft mild goats' cheese) 180 kcals
> 100g rocket or baby salad leaves 25 kcals

For the dressing:

> 1 tbsp olive oil 120 kcals
> 1/2 tbsp balsamic vinegar 3 kcals
> 1/2 tbsp walnut vinegar 3 kcals
> Sea salt and freshly ground black pepper
> 1/2 clove garlic, crushed 2 kcals
> 1/2 tsp grainy mustard 2 kcals

Heat the oven to 200c (fan).

Mix the honey and cinnamon in a bowl and toss the walnuts in the mixture.

Put a non-stick silicone sheet or baking parchment on a baking tray, and spread the nuts over.

Bake in the oven for about 5 minutes, until lightly coloured.

Set aside to cool.

Put the beetroot on a baking tray, drizzle with olive oil and season with salt and pepper.

Cover with foil and bake for 30 - 40 minutes, then set aside to cool.

Turn off the oven and heat up the grill.

Whisk the dressing ingredients together.

Toast the bread and cut in half.

Put the goats' cheese onto a non-stick liner or baking parchment on an oven tray and put under the grill for just a minute or two to warm through and melt slightly.

Put the salad leaves on plates and distribute the beetroot and walnuts.

Slide the goats' cheese onto the toast and put on top of the leaves.

Drizzle the dressing over.

Per serving: kcals 401
Carbs 25g Fat 30g Protein 12g

Salads serve as a nutrient-filled base to a variety of dishes or as zesty and flavourful counterpoint to accompany a main dish... Heaps of lovely green leaves fresh from the garden or market... Wonderful seasonal vegetables, grated, chopped or lightly cooked to add colour and vitamins and minerals.... Decorated with fruit, nuts and seeds to add flavour, crunch and more goodness. Dressed with smooth and silky oils, sharp and tangy citrus juice and enlivened with vinegar.... Cool salads with warm lardons, or melting goats' cheese, drizzled with honey and citrus juices... These salads can be served as starters, as accompaniments or as meals in themselves.

Eating some raw foods every day is good for you as they tend to contain more nutrients and fibre than when cooked and having some foods in their natural state is probably beneficial to your friendly gut bacteria too.

Many of these recipes are suitable for vegetarians.

I hope they give you some good ideas of how to bring variety to your meals and help you to fill your plates with delicious seasonal delights.

Goats Cheese and Runner Beans with Warm Lardons

This is a delicious salad that makes a substantial lunch or light meal. With warm lardons and runner beans (or fine green beans) and some added sweetness in the form of Acacia honey over warm, melting cheese. I usually grill the cabecou separately from the toast as otherwise the bread gets a little too brown at the edges.... This would also work with Camembert.

Serves 1

> **1 Cabecou goats' cheese 90kcals**
>
> **3 radishes, finely sliced 15 kcals**
>
> **1/2 slice wholewheat toast 38 kcals**
>
> **50g runner beans, diagonally sliced 9 kcals**
>
> **50g peeled baby broad beans 43 kcals**
>
> **1 cup mixed salad leaves 13 kcals**
>
> **1 slice of a large onion, cut in half 16 kcals**
>
> **25g smoked bacon lardons 59 kcals**
>
> **1 tsp acacia honey 20 kcals**
>
> **1 tbsp Balsamic and Walnut Vinaigrette (page 124) 26 kcals**

Preheat the grill.

Cook both the beans together in boiling water for just 3 or 4 minutes, so that they are only lightly cooked, and refresh under cold running water (to keep the bright colour), then drain.

Heat a frying pan over medium heat and fry the lardons until slightly browned and most of the fat is rendered out. Lift out with a slotted spoon and drain on kitchen paper and keep warm.

Toast the bread and put the cabecou under the grill on a non-stick tray (ideally on a silicone liner) to soften and warm up.

Arrange the salad leaves with the onion and lardons on a plate. Put the cheese on the toast and lay on top of the salad. Drizzle with the honey.

Scatter the beans and radishes over the top and garnish with the dressing.

Per serving: kcals 329
Carbs 30g Fat 17g Protein 16g

Tuna and Runner Bean Salad

Tuna is one of the lowest-calorie sources of protein and has a wonderful affinity with green beans.

Serves 2

> **100g rocket leaves 18 kcals**
>
> **1/2 red onion, finely sliced 22 kcals**
>
> **1 tin of tuna in spring water, drained 82 kcals**
>
> **200g runner beans, trimmed 46 kcals**
>
> **75g feta cheese, cubed 200 kcals**
>
> **1 stick celery, finely sliced 6 kcals**
>
> **1 tbsp Balsamic and Walnut Vinaigrette (page 124) 26 kcals**

Steam the runner beans for 3 to 4 minutes, until just tender, then refresh under cold water and drain.

Put the dressing into a salad bowl and flake the tuna into it. Add the rocket, onion, beans and celery and gently toss in the dressing.

Distribute the feta cubes on top.

Per serving: kcals 200
Carbs 8g Fat 12g Protein 17g

Green Salad with Seeds

I love to top my salads with some warm, toasted seeds or chopped nuts. Pumpkin seeds are especially tasty, but you could use sunflower seeds or chopped walnuts or hazelnuts for added crunch and protein. Vary the leaves according to what's available and add a little red onion or sliced radishes for contrast. Instead of celery, you could use celeriac, cut into matchsticks or grated. This kind of salad goes very well with a **Crustless Quiche** (page 58) or **Tortilla ~ Spanish Omelette** (page 58).

Serves 2

   1 cup of rocket 6 kcals

   1 cup of lettuce leaves, roughly torn 8 kcals

   1 red onion, sliced 44 kcals

   2 sticks celery, finely sliced 12 kcals

   20g pumpkin seeds, toasted 108 kcals

   2 tbsp Balsamic and Walnut Vinaigrette (page 124) 52 kcals

Toast the pumpkin seeds in a non-stick pan over medium heat, shaking frequently, until golden brown, then set aside to cool.

Toss the leaves with the celery and red onion.

Sprinkle the seeds over all and serve the dressing separately.

Per serving: kcals 105
Carbs 9g Fat 8g Protein 4g

Avocado, Cherry and Walnut

I'm a fan of a little fruit in salads, both fresh and dried. You might think of reaching for some greenhouse grown cherry tomatoes to brighten up a dish - but how about slices of fresh red apples or pears, segments of orange or grapefruit or a few chopped dates or dried apricots instead? Or as here, some luscious semi-sweet cherries, married with toasted walnut halves - this makes a really lively addition to an avocado, tomato and onion salad.

Serves 2

   1 cup of salad leaves 22 kcals

   1/4 cucumber, peeled and sliced 12 kcals

   1 large spring onion, finely sliced 8 kcals

   1 avocado, peeled stoned and cut into segments 396 kcals

   1 large tomato, sliced 32 kcals

   50g cherries, stoned and halved 58 kcals

   25g walnuts, shelled and toasted 154 kcals

   2 tbsp Balsamic and Walnut Vinaigrette (page 124) 52 kcals

Layer all the ingredients into a salad bowl and drizzle the dressing over the top.

This would make a stunning accompaniment to a simple piece of grilled fish or meat or soft cheese with garlic and herbs.

Per serving: kcals 364
Carbs 17g Fat 30g Protein 7g

Tomato and Warm Chorizo Salad

The idea for this came from Jamie Oliver. I love the smoky hot paprika flavour of chorizo and it goes brilliantly well with tomatoes and garlic. Try and get a mix of different colours, sizes and shapes.

Serves 4

500g mixed tomatoes, halved, quartered or sliced, depending on size 88 kcals

1 tbsp extra virgin olive oil 120 kcals

2 tsp sherry vinegar 2 kcals

Sea salt and freshly ground black pepper

200g chorizo, skinned and sliced 912 kcals

2 cloves garlic, peeled and finely sliced 8 kcals

2 or 3 shallots or 1 red onion 44 kcals

A handful of basil, coriander or parsley leaves, finely chopped 1 kcal

To garnish:

A few basil, coriander or parsley leaves

Put the tomatoes into a serving bowl and dress with olive oil and 1 tsp of the vinegar.

Season well with salt and pepper and mix in the chopped herbs.

Cook the chorizo in a frying pan over medium heat, stirring occasionally until it starts to release its oil, then add the sliced garlic and shallots or onions.

Keep stir-frying for a few minutes until the onions have softened and the chorizo is starting to go brown, then remove from the heat and stir in the remaining teaspoon of sherry vinegar.

Toss the chorizo in with the tomatoes and garnish with the chopped herbs.

Per serving: kcals 293 Carbs 9g Fat 23g Protein 14g

You could serve this with Quinoa, Bulgur and Broad Bean Pilaf, or it makes a splendid companion to Dauphinoise Potatoes (page 76), with a green salad alongside.

To make a more substantial dish, mix 400g cooked butter beans (456 kcals) in to the chorizo and warm through, before adding the vinegar.

With butter beans: kcals 406 Carbs 29g Fat 24g Protein 20g

Spanish Style Cauliflower and Caper Salad

I made this to go with sticky pork ribs, which I cooked on the BBQ. The addition of capers and caraway seeds, together with a little smoky paprika, gives the cauliflower an unusual lift out of the ordinary. Based on a recipe in *"Tapas, the little dishes of Spain"* by Penelope Casas.

Serves 2

200g cauliflower florets 50 kcals

Sea salt

1 tsp lemon juice 1 kcal

2 tsp olive oil 80 kcals

2 tsp sherry vinegar 1 kcal

1 clove garlic 4 kcals

1/2 tbsp capers 1 kcal

1/2 tsp caraway seeds 4 kcals

1/2 tsp smoked paprika 4 kcals

Cook the cauliflower florets in boiling salted water to just cover, with the lemon juice added, simmering until just tender, about 10 minutes.

Drain and leave to cool.

Crush the garlic with the caraway seeds and paprika in a pestle and mortar.

Whisk together with the sherry vinegar and olive oil, add the capers and mix with the cauliflower.

Leave to marinade for several hours.

Per serving: kcals 73
Carbs 7g Fat 5g Protein 2g

Heritage Tomato Salad

I so love tomatoes that have been grown in the sunshine. I have experimented with growing lots of different varieties and am particularly fond of this selection - tiny red cherry tomatoes, small orange round ones, dark and non-acidic plum tomatoes or purplish round Russian ones, and large pale beefsteak. Seek out a good variety of colours and shapes to make a simple tomato salad sing and don't forget the salt and pepper. I usually add some sliced onion and chopped basil leaves, then drizzle with extra virgin olive oil and splash with a few drops of aged balsamic vinegar. Summer magic.

Serves 1

> 1 medium tomato 20 kcals
> 1 medium red onion, finely sliced 40 kcals
> 1 tsp olive oil 40 kcals
> 1 tsp aged balsamic vinegar 5 kcals
> Sea salt and freshly ground black pepper

To garnish

> 2 tbsp basil leaves 1 kcal

Halve, slice or quarter the tomatoes and put in a bowl with the onion.

Drizzle over the oil and balsamic vinegar and season well.

Dress with torn basil leaves.

Leave for a little while to allow the flavours to infuse before serving.

Per serving: kcals 108
Carbs 15g Fat 5g Protein 2g

Light Cole Slaw with Cherries

When faced with an abundance of something, it is well worth trying some new ideas…

I was making cole slaw to go with one of our BBQs and usually I add dried fruit, such as raisins, or maybe some chopped apple, but there was this big bowl of fresh cherries in front of me, so I added some of those instead. They added just the right note of acidity and sweetness to contrast with the cabbage, carrots and creamy yogurt and mayo dressing. The borage flowers gave a rather lovely visual lift, I thought.

Serves 4

> 1 tbsp mayonnaise 94 kcals
> 60g natural low fat yogurt 40 kcals
> Juice of 1/2 lemon 6 kcals
> Sea salt and freshly ground black pepper
> 200g white cabbage, grated 52 kcals
> 1 medium carrot, grated 25 kcals
> 100g cherries 64 kcals

To garnish

> Borage flowers or finely chopped chives or spring onion

Mix the mayonnaise with the yogurt and lemon juice and season to taste.

Stir in the cabbage and mix to coat well with the dressing.

Add the cherries on top and decorate with flowers or chopped herbs.

As an alternative to the cherries, you could use 15g raisins or 50g chopped apple.

Per serving: kcals 72
Carbs 10g Fat 3g Protein 2g

Serve with **Oven Baked Scotch Eggs** (page 59).

Chargrilled Courgettes

Here's something to celebrate the start of summer!

Serves 1

> 1 courgette 31 kcals
>
> 1 tsp olive oil 40 kcals
>
> 1 clove garlic, finely chopped 4 kcals
>
> 1/2 red chilli, finely chopped 3 kcals
>
> 1 tbsp lemon juice 3 kcals
>
> 1 cup shredded lettuce 8 kcals
>
> Mint and basil leaves, finely chopped
>
> Sea salt and freshly ground black pepper

Preheat a ridged griddle or pan (I use a Panini toaster).

Slice 1 medium courgette lengthways into 4 slices.

Marinade in a little olive oil with finely chopped garlic and red chilli, then griddle on a ridged pan until tender.

Toss with any remaining marinade mixed with lemon juice, chopped mint and chopped basil.

Season with sea salt and black pepper

Serve at room temperature on a bed of lettuce.

Per serving: kcals 70
Carbs 5g Fat 5g Protein 2g

Would be nice with Parmesan shavings or toasted pine nuts or other nuts/seeds sprinkled over.

Broad Bean and Walnut Salad

I just love the time of year when there are fresh broad beans to pick from the garden! Here is a salad to celebrate them, with a great mixture of flavours and textures. You could use red or white radishes and hazelnuts instead of walnuts.

Serves 2

> 200g broad beans, podded and lightly cooked 146 kcals
>
> 1/2 red onion, finely sliced 22 kcals
>
> 1 large spring onion, finely sliced 8 kcals
>
> 1 long white radish, finely sliced 2 kcals
>
> 25g shelled walnut pieces, toasted 180 kcals
>
> 1 tbsp flat leaf parsley, chopped 2 kcals
>
> 2 tbsp Balsamic and Walnut Vinaigrette (page 124) 52 kcals

Combine all the ingredients and toss together.

Per serving: kcals 206
Carbs 12g Fat 13g Protein 8g

This would work well with a light fresh goat or sheep's cheese, like feta. Serve it with some slivers of Serrano ham and rosette salami, or on a pile of green leaves with some Cantal cheese and sliced tomato.

Flageolet and Guindilla Pepper Salad

You could use any kind of cooked beans like haricot, butter beans (lima or navy beans), borlotti, red kidney - or whole green or puy lentils. They all go well with the flavours of garlic, onion and peppers. These guindilla vasca chillies are a Basque speciality that are bottled in vinegar and are piquant and semi-sweet, rather than searingly hot. Instead of fresh red peppers, you could use bottled red peppers, which are skinned and have a lovely soft texture. So this can easily be a store-cupboard salad, apart from the onion and herbs.

Serves 2

For the dressing

> **1 tbsp extra virgin olive oil 120 kcals**
>
> **1 clove garlic, crushed 4 kcals**
>
> **Juice of 1/2 lemon 6 kcals**
>
> **Handful of mint leaves, finely chopped 2 kcals**
>
> **Sea salt and freshly ground black pepper**

For the salad

> **1 small can flageolets, drained and rinsed 236 kcals**
>
> **1 sweet red pepper, deseeded and finely sliced 36 kcals**
>
> **1 large spring onion, finely sliced 8 kcals**
>
> **4 Guindilla vasca green chilli peppers 8 kcals**

For the garnish

> **A few individual mint leaves**

Put the flageolets, pepper and spring onions and pepper into a serving dish. Whisk together the dressing ingredients and pour over the top.

Garnish with mint leaves.

This salad goes particularly well with an egg-based dish, like a **Tortilla** (page 58) or **Crustless Quiche** (page 58) or serve it with platters of charcuterie and cheeses or perhaps alongside some **Nut Loaf** (page 81) or **Lemony Tuna Kebabs** (page 99).

Per serving: kcals 212
Carbs 26g Fat 7g Protein 9g

Beetroot, Celery and Apple Salad with Tahini Dressing

My mother often made what she called Winter Salad from beetroot, celery and apple. A good combination of flavours and textures. To go with them, I created a dressing from yogurt mixed with tahini. It is interesting how different the eating experience is whether you mix the dressing in thoroughly or leave it separate, so do try both ways. Garnish with a sprinkling of toasted sesame seeds.

Serves 2

> **1 Gala apple, cored and chopped 80 kcals**
>
> **1 stick celery, finely sliced 6 kcals**
>
> **2 beetroot, cooked and chopped 88 kcals**
>
> **125ml natural low fat yogurt 84 kcals**
>
> **1 tbsp tahini sesame paste 100 kcals**
>
> **A squeeze of lemon 6 kcals**

To garnish

> **1 tbsp toasted sesame seeds 52 kcals**
>
> **a few celery leaves, finely chopped**

Mix the yogurt with the lemon juice and tahini.

Either mix the vegetables in with the dressing or serve the dressing on top of the vegetables.

Sprinkle with sesame seeds and garnish with chopped celery leaves

Per serving: kcals 206
Carbs 27g Fat 9g Protein 8g

Raw Vegetable Salad with Vietnamese Dressing

My recipe as published in Kate Harrison's *"The Ultimate 5:2 Diet Recipe Book"*. This initially appeared in *"Focus on Flavour"* - my first cookery book - and was one of the first of those recipes that I put on my 5:2 blog as it is absolutely ideal for a Fast Day. It really does have a bit of zing.

Serves 2

> 1 cup rocket 6 kcals
>
> 50g celeriac, grated or cut in julienne strips 22 kcals
>
> 1/2 red sweet pepper, cut in strips 18 kcals
>
> 1/2 cucumber, sliced diagonally 22 kcals
>
> 1 stick celery, sliced diagonally 6 kcals
>
> 1 carrot, sliced into ribbons 26 kcals
>
> 25g broccoli, small florets 8 kcals
>
> 1 tsp sesame seeds, lightly toasted 18 kcals
>
> Fresh Thai basil or coriander leaves, to garnish

For the dressing

> Juice and grated zest of 1/2 lime 10 kcals
>
> 1/2 tsp sesame oil 20 kcals
>
> 1/2 tsp Thai fish sauce 2 kcals
>
> 1/2 tsp Tamari soy sauce 2 kcals
>
> 1 tsp sweet chilli dipping sauce 12 kcals

Lay all the prepared vegetables on a platter and sprinkle with sesame seeds.

Garnish with basil or coriander.

Whisk together all the dressing ingredients and serve in a dipping bowl.

Other veggies you could use: bean shoots, finely sliced spring onions, raw beetroot strips, courgette ribbons, cauliflower florets, shredded cabbage.

Per serving: kcals 86
Carbs 16g Fat 2g Protein 3g

This also works brilliantly served with sliced white meat from **Asian Poached Chicken** (page 118) or serve with thinly sliced rare steak as a Thai style beef salad, as shown here: -

Raw Vegetable Salad with thinly sliced rare steak

Mushroom and Endive Salad

This makes a pretty salad for the start a meal. You could use little gem lettuce instead of the endive, but the bitterness of the endive contrasts very well with the mushrooms. If I can find them, I like to make it with the red endive (carmine).

Serves 4

> 330g endives, trimmed 56 kcals

300g mushrooms, cleaned and quartered 64 kcals

2 shallots, peeled and finely chopped 16 kcals

10g butter 72 kcals

For the dressing

3 tbsp olive oil 360 kcals

1 tbsp sherry vinegar 3 kcals

1 tsp French Dijon mustard 4 kcal

Sea salt and black pepper

1 tsp cumin seeds 8 kcals

1 tbsp coriander leaves 1 kcal

Melt the butter in a small frying pan and sauté the shallots for a couple of minutes.

Add the mushrooms and season with salt and freshly ground black pepper.

Cook for 5 minutes, then set aside to cool.

Make a dressing by whisking together the olive oil, vinegar and mustard, and season well.

Toast the cumin seeds in a dry frying pan over medium heat for a couple of minutes, shaking from time to time.

Grind coarsely in a pestle and mortar.

Arrange the endives on serving plates and pile some mushrooms into the centre.

Spoon over the dressing and sprinkle with cumin seed.

Garnish with coriander leaves.

Per serving: kcals 145
Carbs 6g Fat 13g Protein 4g

A variation - Lettuce and Endive Salad

Rocket and Orange Salad

Tasty rocket leaves mixed with half an orange, dressed with squeezed orange juice and a few drops of aged balsamic vinegar.

Here with slices of red onion and a few chopped dates and slices of radish.

Serves 2

1/2 orange, juice 19 kcal

1/2 orange, segments 34 kcal

1 tsp aged balsamic vinegar 11 kcals

Sea salt and freshly ground black pepper

1/2 bag (75g) rocket leaves 25 kcal

A few leaves of oak leaf lettuce 9 kcals

1/2 red onion, finely sliced 23 kcals

To garnish:

a couple of radishes, finely sliced 2 kcals

Wash and spin-dry the salad leaves.

Cut the orange in half.

Squeeze one half into a salad bowl and add the balsamic vinegar. Season to taste.

Cut out the segments of the other half of the orange and add to the dressing, along with the onion. At the last minute, add the salad leaves and toss together. Garnish with the radish.

Per serving: kcals 75
Carbs 16g Fat 0g Protein 3g

A very good accompaniment to **Jerusalem Artichoke and Goat's Cheese Gratin** (page 76) or **Skewered Duck with Chilli, Garlic and Hoisin Sauce** (page 113).

Fennel, Citrus and Blue Cheese Salad

Fennel is a great accompaniment for fish. This salad goes particularly well with **Peppered Mackerel with Horseradish Dressing** (page 88).

Serves 4

> 2 fennel bulbs, trimmed and finely sliced 145 kcals
>
> 1 pink grapefruit 41 kcals
>
> 1 small red onion, finely sliced 28 kcals
>
> 35g Roquefort cheese 129 kcals
>
> 2 tsp walnut or sherry vinegar 12 kcals
>
> 1 tbsp flat leaved parsley, chopped
>
> freshly ground black pepper

To garnish

> fennel leaves

Cook the fennel in boiling salted water for 4 minutes, then drain and refresh under cold water.

Cut the grapefruit in half and using a small sharp (or grapefruit) knife, release the segments and set aside, then squeeze the juice into a salad bowl.

Lightly whisk the juice with the cheese and vinegar and season with pepper.

Add the fennel, grapefruit, red onion, and parsley and mix gently.

Garnish with fennel leaves.

Per serving: kcals 89
Carbs 14g Fat 3g Protein 4g

Kachumber Salad

This is the perfect salad to go with spicy Indian style food and introduces the idea of adding spice seeds to enhance everyday ingredients. This goes perfectly with the **Masala Baked Haddock** (page 94).

Serves 2

> 100g baby plum tomatoes, halved or quartered 22 kcals
>
> 1/2 red onion, finely sliced 22 kcals
>
> 1/2 small cucumber, peeled and sliced 22 kcals
>
> 1/2 lime, juice only 5 kcals
>
> 1/2 tsp cumin seed 4 kcals
>
> 1 tbsp coriander leaves, chopped
>
> sea salt

Toast the cumin seeds in a dry frying pan, shaking frequently, until they become fragrant but before they burn.

While the seeds cool, arrange the vegetables on a serving dish.

Crumble a little sea salt over the top and scatter the seeds and coriander leaf over.

Per serving: kcals 45
Carbs 11g Fat 0g Protein 1g

Puy Lentil Salad

The puy lentils are tossed in lime juice, mint and chilli and mixed with red onion, red pepper, tomato and apple. You can vary the flavouring of the puy lentil salad with different fresh herbs, such as basil or coriander. Add a little chopped fresh chilli for a bit of a kick.

Serves 4

    100g puy lentils 104 kcals

    1/2 red onion, finely chopped 24 kcals

    1/2 red pepper, finely chopped 20 kcals

    1 medium tomato, finely chopped 20 kcals

    1 small apple, peeled, cored and chopped 76 kcals

    Juice of 1/2 lime 3 kcals

    40g walnuts, chopped and toasted 248 kcals

    A handful of mint leaves, finely chopped

Cook the puy lentils in six times their volume of cold water, until soft, about 30 minutes.

Drain and rinse with cold water.

Mix together with all the other salad ingredients and set aside.

Per serving: kcals 128
Carbs 15g Fat 6g Protein 5g

Perfect to serve with **Spiced Red Mullet with Coconut-Lime Sauce** (page 95).

Cabbage, Green Pepper and Caraway Salad

This Spanish style salad makes a great change from Cole Slaw having a light dressing, lovely crunch and an excellent combination of flavours. Adapted from *"Tapas, the little dishes of Spain"* by Penelope Casas. I have reduced the amount of olive oil and raisins used in order to make this a light, low-calorie salad that is suitable to use on a 5:2 Fast Day, or on any day as part of a healthy, balanced diet.

Serves 2

    100g white cabbage, finely shredded 25 kcals

    1 medium carrot, cut in fine julienne strips 25 kcals

    1/2 green pepper, cut in fine julienne strips 12 kcals

    10g raisins 30 kcals

For the dressing

    1/2 tbsp extra virgin olive oil 60 kcals

    1/2 tbsp white wine vinegar 2 kcal

    1/2 tsp Dijon mustard 2 kcals

    Sea salt

    Freshly ground black pepper

For the garnish

    1/2 tsp caraway seeds 3 kcals

Put the shredded vegetables in a serving dish. Whisk the dressing ingredients together and season to taste with salt and pepper. Pour the dressing over the salad and toss well. Sprinkle the caraway seeds over the top.

Per serving: kcals 70
Carbs 12g Fat 4g Protein 2g

Serve with **Chicken with Garlic and Saffron** (page 121) and **Potatoes with Spicy Tomato Sauce** (page 78).

Caraway Seeds contain a variety of vitamins, minerals, essential oils and anti-oxidants with many potential health benefits.

They go particularly well with cabbage, as their anti-flatulent properties are considered to be helpful.

Light Caesar Salad

Lighten the dressing by using yogurt along with some mayonnaise. Then instead of garnishing with fried croutons, use some crispy air-dried ham A great idea that was suggested in *"The Fast Diet"* by Dr Michael Mosley and Mimi Spencer.

Serves 2

> 3 slices (30g) Bayonne Ham (Prosciutto) 75 kcals
>
> 2 cups romaine lettuce 15 kcals
>
> 10g Parmesan cheese 32 kcals
>
> 100g plain low-fat yogurt 54 kcals
>
> 2 anchovy fillets, chopped 17 kcals
>
> 1 tbsp mayonnaise 57 kcals
>
> 1/2 lemon, juice 6 kcals

Cook the ham under a hot grill for just a minute or two, until crisp.

Drain on kitchen paper.

To make the dressing, put the yogurt, mayonnaise, lemon juice and anchovies into a food processor and whizz until creamy and smooth.

Pour into a salad bowl.

Wash and spin-dry the lettuce and cut into shreds then toss with the dressing.

Grate the Parmesan cheese over and crumble the ham on top.

A wonderful starter or light lunch, or can be made more substantial by adding some slices of Asian Poached Chicken.

Per serving: kcals 128
Carbs 8g Fat 6g Protein 11g

Fennel and Radish Salad

A classic Italian duo, finely sliced fennel combined with finely sliced radishes. Add some rocket to give the colour contrast and dressed simply with lemon juice and fennel leaves. Goes very well with **Ham and Leek Stuffed Pancakes** (page 108) as well as with cold roast pork or smoked mackerel.

A few toasted pine nuts on top would be a tasty addition.

Serves 2

> 1 fennel bulb, finely sliced 73 kcals
>
> 6 radishes, finely sliced 4 kcals
>
> a handful of rocket leaves
>
> Juice of 1 lemon 12 kcals

To garnish

> A few fennel leaves

Per serving: kcals 45
Carbs 12g Fat 0g Protein 2g

Beanshoot Salad

A simple sesame dressing makes the most of light and crunchy fresh beanshoots, full of vitality. Perfect to serve with **Chicken Satay** (page 112).

Serves 4

> 300g beanshoots, rinsed 39 kcals
>
> 1/2 red pepper, deseeded and cut in strips 18 kcals
>
> 1 tbsp Tamari soy sauce 11 kcals
>
> 1 tbsp tahini 89 kcals
>
> a few drops of sesame oil 20 kcals
>
> a handful of coriander leaves

Mix the Tamari and tahini together with a few drops of sesame oil.

Toss the beanshoots and red pepper in the dressing and garnish with coriander leaves.

Per serving: kcals 44
Carbs 4g fat 3g Protein 2g

As a variation, you might like to add a squeeze of lemon or orange juice and a sprinkling of toasted sesame seeds.

Greek Salad with Feta and Olives

Making a salad like this always brings me happy memories - of holidays in Cyprus or meals at one of our favourite Greek restaurants in London. Of course it goes wonderfully well with **Lemony Lamb Skewers** (page 106) or **Lemony Tuna Kebabs** (page 99). No need to make a complicated dressing for a salad like this - a drizzle of fruity extra virgin olive oil and a squeeze of lemon is all you need.

Serves 2

> 1 Little Gem lettuce or romaine heart 15 kcals
>
> 1/2 cucumber, peeled and cut into chunks 23 kcals
>
> 2 large or 4 medium tomatoes, sliced or halved 52 kcals
>
> 1/2 onion, sliced 22 kcals
>
> 50g feta cheese 132 kcals
>
> 8 black kalamata olives 45 kcals
>
> 1 tbsp flat leaved parsley leaves, chopped
>
> 2 tsp olive oil 80 kcals
>
> 2 lemon wedges 4 kcals

Per serving: kcals 186
Carbs 15g Fat 13g Protein 6g

Roast Pumpkin and Glazed Walnut Salad

Glorious colour to brighten up an autumn or winter day. This would be very good with some bacon lardons running through it, or topped with chopped feta or blue cheese or slices of taleggio. You could also dress it with toasted pumpkin seeds.

Serves 2

> **300g pumpkin, peeled and cubed 102 kcals**
>
> **1/2 tbsp sunflower oil 62 kcals**
>
> **1/2 tsp aged balsamic vinegar 3 kcals**
>
> **Sea salt and freshly ground black pepper**
>
> **25g walnut pieces 155 kcals**
>
> **1 tbsp maple syrup 52 kcals**
>
> **2 tbsp walnut or cider vinegar 6 kcals**
>
> **75g rocket leaves 19 kcals**

Preheat the oven to 180c (fan).

Put the cubes of pumpkin on a baking sheet, drizzle with oil and vinegar and season with salt and pepper.

Roast for 25 - 30 minutes, until the pumpkin is soft and starting to brown.

Heat the maple syrup and vinegar in a small pan until they are well combined then toss the walnut pieces in to coat thoroughly.

Dress the rocket with the pumpkin and walnuts, drizzling over any remaining dressing.

Serve warm.

Per serving: kcals 199
Carbs 22g Fat 12g Protein 6g

Eggs are brilliant food for a fast day, especially if you like to have breakfast - there is nothing nicer than starting the day with a boiled egg, perhaps with asparagus spears to dip into it - or scrambled eggs with smoked fish or lean ham on the side. It is the ideal food when you need to make something quick and easy.

1 large egg has only 75 calories but contains 6g of protein, so it helps you to feel full and satisfied.

Always choose organic, free-range eggs; then you can be sure that the chickens have been well fed and well cared-for.

*Tip: Boiling Eggs. To avoid getting a dark ring around the yolk, as soon as the eggs are done, drain the pan and immediately put under cold running water, until well cooled.

Veggie Pops

This year I had an abundance of patty pan (summer) squash. I started making a kind of rosti cake with them. They were very popular, but it was awkward to cook more than a couple at a time. So I hit on the idea of using a silicon mini tart mould and baking them in the oven. Much easier and look neater too. You could any kind of squash, such as courgette or pumpkin and try adding different vegetables - carrot, celeriac or sweet potato - and various herbs and spices too.

Serves 2

180g patty pan squash 28 kcals

10g ground almonds 61 kcals

1 large egg, lightly beaten 75 kcals

1 fresh green chilli, finely chopped 2 kcals

1 tbsp grated Parmesan 22 kcals

Sea salt and freshly ground black pepper

Preheat oven to 180c.

Grate the squash into a clean cloth and wring out as much liquid as you can.

Combine all the ingredients together in a bowl and season well with salt and pepper

Transfer to silicone moulds (should make 4) and press down well.

Bake in the centre of the oven for about 15 minutes until golden.

Remove from the moulds and serve immediately.

Per serving: kcals 94
Carbs 4g Fat 6g Protein 5g

Smoked Trout and Scrambled Egg

A quick and easy fast day breakfast

Serves 1

45g or 65g smoked trout (or smoked salmon) 85 or 117 kcals

1 or 2 large eggs 75 or 150 kcals

Freshly ground black pepper

A wedge of lemon (optional, to serve)

Use the best eggs you can get, preferably organic free-range.

Use a good non-stick pan for the eggs and you won't need to add any butter.

Break the eggs into a jug, whisk lightly with a fork, season with freshly ground black pepper.

Cook the eggs quickly, stirring often and turning off the heat just before they are fully cooked, as they will continue cooking with the residual heat.

You can either cut the trout into pieces and mix in with the egg just before serving, or serve the slices with a wedge of lemon.

1 egg, 45g smoked trout:

Small serving: kcals 160
Carbs 1g Fat 9g Protein 18g

2 eggs, 65g smoked trout:

Large serving: kcals 267
Carbs 1g Fat 15g Protein 30g

Tortilla ~ Spanish Omelette

I sometimes forget how delicious and simple a frittata, tortilla or Spanish omelette can be. It's a great way of using up leftovers and oddments of vegetables and cooked meats too. If you like the traditional smooth shape of a tortilla, you need to transfer it to a plate and turn it over several times during the cooking.

Serves 2

> **1/2 tbsp sunflower oil 60 kcals**
> **1 onion, finely chopped 44 kcals**
> **35g chorizo, cut in small cubes 159 kcals**
> **1 slice lean ham, cut in small cubes 30 kcals**
> **40g button mushrooms, quartered 9 kcals**
> **50g courgette, diced 8 kcals**
> **30g red pepper, diced 9 kcals**
> **4 large organic eggs 286 kcals**
> **Sea salt and freshly ground black pepper**
> **1 tbsp flat leaf parsley, finely chopped 1 kcal**
> **30g grated cheese 121 kcals**
> **5g unsalted butter 36 kcals**

Break the eggs into a large jug and beat lightly with a fork.

Season with salt and pepper and add the parsley.

Heat the sunflower oil in a frying pan and gently sauté the onion until starting to soften and become translucent.

Toss in the chorizo, mushrooms, courgette and red pepper, stir-fry gently for about 5 minutes, then add the ham.

Mix together with the eggs and stir in the grated cheese.

Melt the butter in an omelette pan over medium-low heat until it starts to get frothy, making sure that the pan is completely coated in butter.

Pour the egg mixture into the pan and leave to cook for about a couple of minutes, then start to loosen the mix from the sides.

When the base is fairly well set, put a flat plate upside down over the pan and then invert the pan and plate together to transfer the tortilla to the plate.

Then slide the tortilla off the plate back into the pan.

Allow to cook for a couple more minutes and do the same thing again.

This gives a lovely rounded shape, which can be easily cut into portions.

Continue until the tortilla is cooked to your liking - I prefer to have the middle still just slightly soft - then slide out of the pan onto a serving plate.

Serve with a side salad.

Per serving: kcals 383
Carbs 9g Fat 28g Protein 25g

Crustless Asparagus and Salmon Quiche

It is really quite surprising how successful a crustless quiche is - you really don't need the pastry. This is also a useful way to use any leftover cooked fish, or you could use smoked salmon, which gives it a wonderful flavour.

Serves 3

> **1/2 tsp vegetable oil 20 kcals**

3 large eggs 225 kcals

10 green or white asparagus spears 40 kcals

175 ml soya or dairy milk 130 kcals

50g Cantal or other well-flavoured hard cheese, grated 193 kcals

150g salmon fillet 237 kcals

1 tbsp flat leaf parsley, finely chopped

Sea salt and freshly ground black pepper

Preheat the oven to 160c (fan).

Snap the asparagus as near to the base as possible and discard the ends.

If using white asparagus, peel off the outer skin with a peeler or sharp knife.

Steam the asparagus spears for 5 - 6 minutes, until just tender.

Drain and leave until cool enough to handle.

Meanwhile, wrap the fish in baking parchment and bake in the oven for 15 minutes, or grill until just cooked. Separate into large flakes. If using smoked salmon, cut into strips.

Brush or spray a little oil on the inside of a quiche dish.

Distribute the salmon over the base of the dish.

Trim the asparagus to fit the radius of the dish and lay evenly around with the points towards the centre.

Use any trimmings to fill the gaps.

Sprinkle the grated cheese evenly over the top.

Break the eggs into a jug, beat well, stir in the milk and season well (you will not really need any salt if using smoked salmon).

Pour over the salmon and asparagus, then garnish with the chopped parsley.

Bake in the centre of the oven for 30 - 40 minutes, until lightly golden brown and set in the middle.

Serve hot, warm or cold.

Per serving: kcals 282
Carbs 4g Fat 12g Protein 20g

This is really excellent if served with a good drizzle of **Gremolata** (page 96).

Oven Baked Scotch Eggs

Ah memories of summer picnics... a great way to take sausage and egg with you, or enjoy eating in the garden on a fine day. Coated in a mix of breadcrumbs and crumbled crispbread and baked in the oven, these are lighter than traditional fried Scotch eggs.

Serves 4

4 large eggs, lightly hard boiled and shelled (see Tip on page 55) 280 kcals

400g lean minced pork sausage-meat 460 kcals

1 large egg, beaten 70 kcals

15g plain flour 52 kcals

Herbes de Provence (or other herbs or spices)

40g wholewheat breadcrumbs 85 kcals

1 crispbread, crumbled or crushed with a rolling pin 35 kcals

Sea salt and freshly ground black pepper

Preheat oven to 180c (fan)

Make sure your eggs are cooked firmly enough so that you can take the shells off, but not too hard - as they will get extra cooking later.

Prepare 3 bowls - one with seasoned flour, one with beaten egg, one with the breadcrumbs and crispbread mixed together

Roll the eggs in a little flour.

Add the herbs and some seasoning to the sausage-meat, then divide up and flatten each piece between damp hands and then wrap around the eggs, pressing the joins together so that there are no gaps.

Then with each egg in turn, roll in the flour, shake off any excess, then dip in the beaten egg, turning until completely coated, then lift out with a slotted spoon or a fork and dip in the breadcrumbs and roll until nicely covered.

Put on a non-stick baking sheet, or one covered with baking parchment or a silicone liner, and bake for about 25 - 30 minutes until nicely golden and crisped on the outside.

Serve while still slightly warm, or allow to cool completely, then refrigerate until serving.

They go really well with Light Coleslaw or a Beetroot, Celery and Apple Salad.

Per serving: kcals 390 Carbs 10g Fat 24g Protein 34g

Smoked Haddock with Poached Egg and Wilted Spinach

I noticed that the fish counter in a local supermarket had smoked haddock. Something of a treat for us here in South West France! An easy and quick to prepare, protein-rich, satisfying fast day main course.

Serves 1

> **100 or 125g smoked haddock fillet 116 or 145 kcals**
>
> **5g unsalted butter 36 kcals**
>
> **1 or 2 large eggs 74 or 148 kcals**
>
> **1 cup of spinach leaves 13 kcals**
>
> **A pinch of grated nutmeg**
>
> **Freshly ground black pepper**

Wash the spinach and put into a saucepan with the water that clings to it.

Season with grated nutmeg and black pepper, then cook gently over a low heat until wilted.

Remove the skin from the fish, if you wish.

Put enough water to cover the fish into a pan and bring to the boil. Add the fish and cook at a gentle simmer for 3-4 minutes, depending on thickness of the fillet.

Meanwhile, poach your egg to your liking - I use poaching cups and use a little butter to stop the eggs sticking to them.

Any remaining butter can be used to dress the spinach.

Small serving: kcals 233 Carbs 1g Fat 10g Protein 32g

Large serving: kcals 335 Carbs 2g Fat 15g Protein 46g

Ham, Egg and Chips

Now you don't need a recipe for this! But I wanted to include it, as it is something that we have occasionally and why not? A modest portion of oven baked French fries makes an enjoyable addition.

Serves 1

> **1 or 2 large fried eggs 92 / 184 kcals**
>
> **1 or 2 slices ham 32 / 64 kcals**
>
> **100g oven French fries 158 kcals**

Small serving: kcals 282 Carbs 29g Fat 12g Protein 15g

Large serving: kcals 406 Carbs 29g Fat 20g Protein 27g

Egg Curry, with Spinach and Mung Beans

You can usually find mung beans in a health food shop, small green beans, which are grown as bean sprouts. Or in this recipe you could substitute with lentils, which also do not require a long pre-soaking. I learned a lot about using spices from *"Indian Vegetarian Cookery"* by Jack Santa Maria and this dish seems to have evolved from several recipes. You could add rice at the same time as the beans to make this more like a traditional Bengali khichuri.

Serves 3

1 cup mung beans 212 kcals

1 tbsp sunflower oil or ghee 120 kcals

1 onion, chopped 46 kcals

2.5 cm root ginger, finely chopped 10 kcals

1 clove garlic, chopped 4 kcals

1 tsp ground turmeric 8 kcals

1/2 tsp chilli powder 5 kcals

12 black peppercorns

4 cloves

4 cardamom pods, crushed to release the seeds

2 tsp cumin seeds 16 kcals

2.5cm piece of cinnamon stick

3 plum tomatoes, skinned and chopped 33 kcals

3 large eggs 233 kcals

100ml light coconut milk 130 kcals

200 ml water

100g leaf spinach, chopped 28 kcals

Sea salt

To garnish

1 tsp garam masala and some chopped coriander leaves

Wash the mung beans and leave to soak in cold water for at least 30 minutes (if your beans have been lurking in the back of the cupboard for a year or more, it's better to soak them overnight...)

Pound the ginger, garlic, turmeric, chilli, peppercorns, cloves and cardamom seeds in a pestle and mortar.

Heat the oil in a heavy pan and lightly fry the onion until translucent. Add the masala paste, together with the cumin seeds and cinnamon stick. Fry for a few minutes, adding a little water if needed to stop it burning, then add the drained mung beans and tomatoes.

Fry for a few more minutes then add the coconut milk and water and bring to the boil.

Lower heat, cover with a lid and simmer until the beans are cooked through, adding a little water if necessary.

Meanwhile put the eggs into cold water, bring to the boil and simmer for 8 minutes, then cool under running water.

Peel and halve the eggs.

Add the spinach to the curry and cook until wilted, then gently add the eggs to the top and serve with a garnish of chopped coriander leaf and a sprinkle of garam masala.

Per serving: kcals 397 kcals
Carbs 34g fat 20g protein 21g

Serve with **Cucumber Raita** (page 126), **Tomato, Red Onion and Coriander Chutney** (page 126) and **Naan Bread** (page 128).

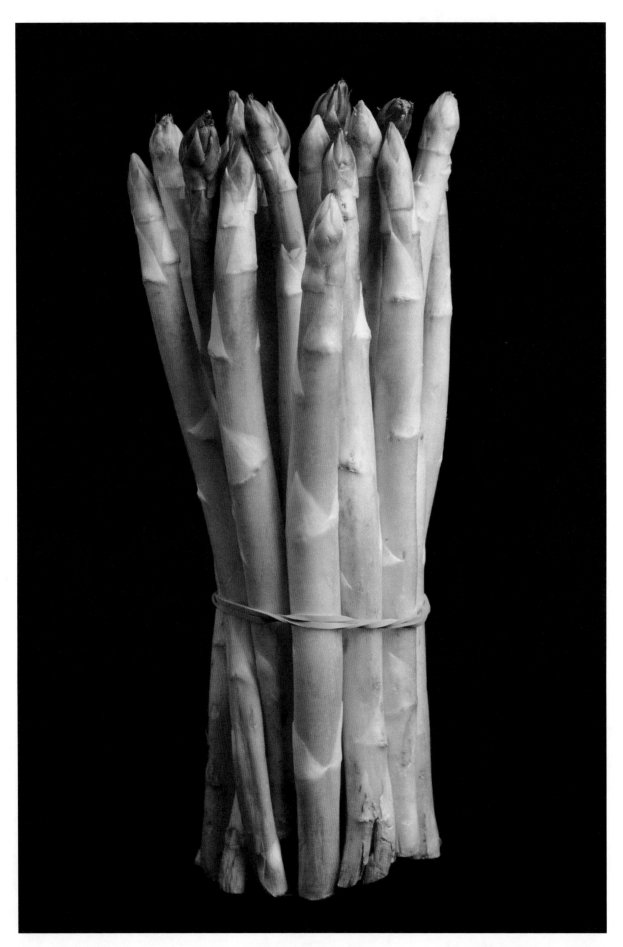

Pastry

Once upon a time I used rich buttery pastry quite frequently - so easy, when the ready rolled pastry is so good here in France! I still use it occasionally as a treat, but I have found that Filo (phyllo) pastry is a great ally to anyone wanting to lose weight or keep their meals light and low in starchy carbohydrates but wanting a container, a topping, a change of texture...

Because it is made without the use of fat, Filo is much lower in calories than standard pastry.

When using layers, it helps to brush a little oil or melted butter to help keep them separate, but I have found that I can be really frugal by just brushing half a sheet, then folding to spread the oil on the other half, put the next sheet on top, then lift that and turn it over - doing it like that uses one quarter of the fat that would have been used otherwise. I have also found that filo behaves surprisingly well without being brushed with butter or oil at all, but obviously you can do so if you don't mind the extra calories!

In this section you will only find savoury recipes using filo - there are some lovely ways to use it for desserts as well, which you will find in the Desserts section.

Spring Vegetables with Sesame Wafers

Fresh lightly cooked broad beans and petit pois, combined with cucumber, apple and bean shoots. Dressed with Tamari soy sauce, lemon juice and toasted sesame oil and topped with wafers of filo pastry and sesame seeds. This makes a great starter for a dinner party and can easily be adapted to suit a variety of vegetables.

Serves 4

2 sheets filo pastry 164 kcals

2 tsp sesame seeds 36 kcals

1 tsp olive oil 40 kcals

100g broad beans 72 kcals

100g peas 80 kcals

1/2 cucumber, diced 24 kcals

100g beanshoots 28 kcals

2 tsp Tamari soy sauce 8 kcals

2 tsp lemon juice 4 kcals

Freshly ground black pepper

To garnish

4 slices cucumber, halved

Mint leaves

Heat the oven to 180c (fan).

Brush half a sheet of filo very lightly with olive oil, fold the other half over to transfer the oil, then open out again. Lay the other sheet on top and then turn it over. Cut the sheet in half, lay one half on top of the other, then repeat and cut into rectangles.

Separate the stacks so that they are just 3 layers each and put them onto a lightly greased baking sheet, or on a sheet with a non-stick liner.

Sprinkle with sesame seeds.

To keep flat while baking, cover with a sheet of baking parchment and top with another baking sheet.

Bake in the oven for about 10 minutes, until crisp and golden.

Meanwhile, cook the broad beans and peas in boiling salted water until tender, about 4 minutes, refresh with cold water, then drain and leave to cool.

Put the soy sauce and lemon juice in a bowl, add the vegetables and mix together gently. Season with black pepper.

Make a tidy pile of vegetables in the centre of each plate (use a ring for neatness), top with a filo wafer and garnish with a couple of pieces of cucumber and some mint leaves.

Vary the vegetables through the seasons and use different herbs and spices to ring the changes, always aiming for a mix of textures.

Per serving: kcals 120
Carbs 18g Fat 3g Protein 6g

Asparagus Filo Spears

Asparagus Filo Spears

As asparagus has such a short season, I try to make the most of it. This makes a cute starter or can be served as an appetizer. I have found that filo behaves surprisingly well without being brushed with butter or oil, but obviously you can do so if you don't mind the extra calories!

Serves 4

> **4 sheets filo pastry 328 kcals**
> **16 stems green asparagus 76 kcals**
> **1 tsp olive oil 40 kcals**
> **2 tbsp grated Parmesan 44 kcals**

Preheat the oven to 180c (fan).

Snap the asparagus as close to the bottom as it will allow. Cook in boiling salted water for 2 to 3 minutes, until just tender, then drain and pat dry.

Cut each sheet of filo into 4 strips widthways (so they are short and fat, rather than long and thin).

Place an asparagus spear on a strip and roll up at a slight angle, leaving the tip exposed. Repeat for all the asparagus.

Lay on a lightly greased or non-stick baking sheet, with the end of the pastry underneath, so that it doesn't unroll. Brush very lightly with olive oil and sprinkle most of the Parmesan over the top - reserve some for serving.

Bake towards to top of the oven for about 10 minutes, until golden. Sprinkle with the remaining Parmesan and serve.

Per serving: kcals 120
Carbs 19g Fat 3g Protein 5g

A little sweet chilli dipping sauce makes a tasty accompaniment, as shown on previous page.

Asparagus and Cheese Pockets

I love asparagus and like to find different ways to serve it, as I could eat it every day during its short season. You can use either green or white asparagus and in fact I used two of each here. I find that the white asparagus needs to be peeled though, which makes it rather time consuming to prepare and I do really prefer the flavour and texture of the green. For the cheese, I chose Comté, but any nutty-flavoured Swiss style cheese, would do the job.

Serves 4

> **2 sheets filo pastry 164 kcals**
> **4 tsp grainy mustard 12 kcals**
> **16 stems asparagus 76 kcals**
> **4 tbsp grated Comté 112 kcals**
> **Sea salt and freshly ground black pepper**
> **A little olive oil for brushing 40 kcals**

For serving

> **1 bunch of watercress 10 kcals**
> **6 small tomatoes 96 kcals**
> **2 tbsp Balsamic and Walnut Vinaigrette (page 124) 52 kcals**

Preheat the oven to 180c (fan).

Snap the asparagus as close to the bottom as it will allow and remove the tough outer layer with a peeler, if using white asparagus. Place in a steamer basket over boiling water, cover with a lid and cook for 4 minutes. Remove from the heat and refresh under cold running water, drain, then put onto kitchen paper to dry.

Lay one sheet of filo on top of the other and cut into 4 squares.

Trim the asparagus so that it is shorter than the diagonal length of the square (keep any trimmings to use in a soup or salad).

Spread a teaspoonful of mustard in the centre of each square and top with 4 asparagus spears, with their tips close to one corner. Sprinkle a spoonful of cheese over each one and season with salt and pepper. Brush a little oil over the exposed pastry.

Fold one corner of the pastry over the bottom of the stems and then wrap the two sides over each other. Lay onto a non-stick baking sheet, or one covered with a liner and brush very lightly with oil. Bake towards the top of the oven for 8 - 10 minutes, until golden.

Serve with immediately with a crisp green salad - peppery watercress makes a flavoursome partner - and drizzle some dressing over the plate.

Per serving: kcals 150
Carbs 19g Fat 6g Protein 6g

You could sprinkle poppy, sesame or mixed seeds for baking over the pastry before cooking, for decoration. For an elegant starter, a spoonful of hollandaise or mousseline sauce would be a good match.

Spanakopitta - Spinach and Feta Filo Pastries

These Greek-inspired spinach and feta pastries are a delicious treat for any day of the week!

Because filo pastry is fat free, you can get the lovely crispness of pastry without loads of calories.

They are not difficult to make as individual triangles, but if you prefer you could make one large pie using the four sheets of pastry overlapping each other.

Makes 16 - Serves 4

- **2 cups spinach leaves 14 kcals**
- **100g feta cheese, chopped or crumbled 288 kcals**
- **1 large egg, beaten 70 kcals**
- **2 tbsp coriander leaves finely chopped 7 kcals**
- **1 tbsp olive oil 120 kcals**
- **4 sheets filo pastry 328 kcals**
- **A pinch of nutmeg**
- **Freshly ground black pepper**

Heat oven to 200c (fan).

Heat 1/2 tbsp oil in a frying pan and gently sauté the shallots or onion until softened but not coloured.

Wash the spinach well and put into a saucepan with the water that clings to it. Cover and cook gently until tender.

Strain through a sieve, pressing out all the liquid, then turn out onto a board and chop roughly.

Put the spinach into a bowl and add the shallots, feta cheese, beaten egg, coriander leaves, freshly grated nutmeg and black pepper and mix well.

Work with one single sheet of filo pastry at a time, keeping the remainder wrapped up.

Cut the sheet of pastry into 4 equal long strips.

Add a spoonful of spinach mixture at one end and turn into triangles. Put onto a lightly oiled baking sheet.

Continue until the mixture is used up - it should be enough to make 16.

Brush the outside of the pastries very lightly with olive oil. Bake for about 10 minutes until golden.

Serve with a mixed salad with black olives.

Per pastry: kcals 49
Carbs 5g Fat 3g Protein 2g

Per serving: kcals 196
Carbs 18g Fat 11g Protein 8g

Tomato and Feta Filo Tart

This recipes combines some of my favourite summer ingredients – tomatoes and basil, with filo pastry and feta cheese – to make a delightful starter when entertaining, or a yummy fast day meal. Celebrate summer and luscious ripe tomatoes!

Serves 4 as a main course or 8 as a starter

6 sheets filo pastry 494 kcals
1.5 tbsp olive oil 179 kcals
2 tbsp pesto 135 kcals
100g feta cheese, crumbled 264 kcals
6 large tomatoes, sliced 197 kcals
salt and pepper
12 basil leaves

Preheat oven to 210c (fan).

Line a large baking sheet with a piece of baking parchment (facilitates removal of the tart later!)

Lay as sheet of filo on the paper and brush lightly with oil.

Lay another sheet of pastry on top, then lift and turn over (this helps to use much less oil than brushing each sheet)

Repeat until all 6 sheets of pastry have been used.

Turn over the edges to make a neat outer rim.

Brush the pesto evenly over the top, then crumble over half of the feta cheese.

Arrange the tomato slices over the top

Season with salt and pepper and sprinkle over the remaining feta cheese.

Bake until the pastry is crisp and golden, about 30 minutes.

Cool in the pan then transfer to a board.

Scatter the basil over, then slice and serve warm or cool, with crisp salad leaves.

As a starter: kcals 160
Carbs 19g Fat 8g Protein 5g

As a main: kcals 318
Carbs 38g Fat 15g Protein 10g

We eat lots of vegetables, especially on fast days - they help to fill your plate and keep you well nourished and of course they feature as accompaniments to all the main dishes. But sometimes vegetables become the stars of the show and here are some recipes that really make them shine.

Many of these main dishes are ideal for vegetarians but everyone should be looking to get more of their protein from plant based sources - that means nuts, seeds, beans and lentils and grains like quinoa, plus products like tofu (pressed bean curd made from soy beans). Most vegetables have at least some protein and also varying amounts of carbohydrates, with root vegetables being top of the list.

Try to include all parts of vegetables in your daily intake - roots, stems, leaves, fruits and seeds (seeds, grains or nuts) in order to get the widest range of nutrients and trace elements.

Steaming vegetables, rather than boiling or microwaving them, is better for helping to retain as much of the nutrients as possible, especially vitamin C and folic acid. Some vegetables, such as tomatoes, actually increase the availability of phyto-nutrients after having been cooked, but in general a short cooking time is preferable.

Leek Risotto with Parmesan Crisps

My method of making risotto is based on Nigel Slater's recipe in *"Tender"*. A good stock is an important part of a risotto as the rice absorbs all the flavour. You could vary this by adding cooked peas or mange tout just before the end of the cooking, and garnish with a little grated lemon zest or finely sliced fresh sorrel.

Serves 2, or 4-6 as a starter

> **2 leeks 108 kcals**
>
> **20g unsalted butter 144 kcals**
>
> **120g Arborio rice 444 kcals**
>
> **175ml dry white wine 144 kcals**
>
> **500ml (2 cups) of hot, well-flavoured, vegetable or chicken stock 20 kcals**
>
> **Sea salt and black pepper**
>
> **1 batch of Parmesan crisps 48 kcals**

Put the butter and leeks into a large shallow pan over low heat and cook gently, stirring occasionally, until the leeks are wonderfully soft, but not coloured, which will take about 15 minutes.

Then add the rice and stir it in so that it is coated with the butter.

Add the wine and let it bubble until it has almost disappeared.

Gradually add the hot stock, a couple of ladlefuls at a time, stir, leave to get mostly absorbed, then add some more and continue this way, stirring and adding liquid, so that it never gets dry.

After about 20 minutes, the rice should have swollen and become creamy but still have a little firmness.

Meanwhile, be baking the Parmesan crisps in the oven.

Season with salt and pepper and serve with the Parmesan Crisps.

Per serving kcals 454
Carbs 65g Fat 11g Protein 9g

Parmesan Crisps

These are perfect with Leek Risotto. I used to make them in a frying pan, but found my success rate was very variable and they were time consuming to do. I then discovered that they work brilliantly if you bake them in the oven. These are so delicious; they really bring a risotto to life!

Serves 2

> **15g (2 heaped tbsp) Parmesan cheese 48 kcals**

Preheat the oven to 180c.

Grate the Parmesan cheese finely and drop teaspoonfuls onto a baking sheet covered with a non-stick liner.

Flatten the heaps gently.

Bake for about 5 minutes, until melted.

After they have cooled a little, lift them with a spatula then drape them over a rolling pin to give a nice curved shape, until they have set.

These can be made a little ahead of when you need them.

Perfect with Leek Risotto, or could be served as an elegant and more-ish appetiser.

Per serving: kcals 24
Carbs 0g Fat 2g Protein 2g

Quinoa, Bulgur and Broad Bean Pilaf

Quinoa (pronounced keen-wah) is one of todays superfoods, as it contains the whole chain of amino acids, making it a complete protein source. The grains are in fact seeds of a plant that is native to South America. It takes on flavours well and is quite quick to cook. I have used Quinoa Gourmand for this recipe, which is a mix of red and white quinoa with bulgur wheat. I was inspired to create this after reading Yotam Ottolenghi's *Cookbook*.

Serves 2 as a side dish

60g Quinoa and Bulgur mix 210 kcals

Boiling salted water

2 tsp olive oil 80 kcals

1/2 medium onion, finely sliced 22 kcals

2 cloves garlic, finely chopped 8 kcals

40g young broad beans 34 kcals

1/2 sweet red bell pepper, chopped 15 kcals

To garnish:

1 tbsp leaf coriander/cilantro, finely chopped

20g walnut pieces, toasted 131 kcals

Cook the quinoa in plenty of boiling salted water for 12 minutes, then drain.

Simmer the beans in a small pan of boiling water for 3-5 minutes until just tender, then drain.

Heat the oil in a frying pan and gently sauté the onion and garlic until softened.

Add the pepper and stir-fry for a few minutes until tender.

Add the drained cooked quinoa and the cooked broad beans and mix gently.

Garnish with chopped coriander and toasted walnuts.

This would be lovely with some grilled Halloumi cheese or topped with a poached egg and works well as a supporting act for Baked Jerk Spiced Chicken.

Per serving: kcals 253
Carbs 28g Fat 13g Protein 8g

Bayonne-wrapped Pumpkin

This makes an interesting starter, to serve with a little celeriac remoulade or cole slaw alongside.

As a side dish, the salty tang of air-dried ham goes particularly well with fish or chicken.

Serves 2

2 wedges of pumpkin, peeled and deseeded (150g flesh) 51 kcals

2 slice of air-dried ham (Bayonne, prosciutto) 41 kcals

Cut each slice of ham in half lengthwise and cut the pumpkin wedges into two halves.

Wrap the pumpkin with the ham and place on a baking sheet.

Cook in the oven for about 30 minutes, until the pumpkin is tender and the ham crispy.

Per serving: kcals 46
Carbs 6g Fat 1g Protein 4g

I served this alongside **Salmon Baked with Pesto** (page 94).

Wholewheat Pasta with Sprouting Broccoli and Chilli

As we generally have cut back on refined carbohydrates I was particularly pleased to find some fresh organic wholewheat tagliatelle to use for this dish, but it works well with bows or other small pasta shapes. I came across the original recipe for this in Delicious magazine and it has become a firm favourite as a way to make the most of sprouting or tenderstem broccoli. You could use less olive oil, but it adds a lot to the flavour and also helps to lower the Glycaemic Index of the dish, as does the Parmesan.

Serves 3

> **200g sprouting broccoli 72 kcals**
>
> **1 tbsp olive oil 120 kcals**
>
> **1 clove garlic, finely chopped 4 kcals**
>
> **1 red or green chilli, seeds removed, finely chopped or 1/2 tsp dried chilli flakes 1 kcal**
>
> **250g wholewheat tagliatelle 700 kcals**
>
> **Sea salt and freshly ground black pepper**

To garnish

> **25g Parmesan, cut into slivers 100 kcals**

Cut the broccoli stems into 5cm lengths and set the heads to one side.

Heat the olive oil in a large frying pan over medium heat and then toss in the garlic and chilli.

Stir-fry very gently for a couple of minutes then add the broccoli stems.

Cook these for a few minutes then add the heads and cook for another few minutes, depending on thickness, 5 - 7 minutes in total.

Meanwhile cook the pasta in plenty of boiling water according to the packet instructions.

Drain the pasta, reserving a couple of spoonfuls of the cooking water.

Mix the pasta in to the broccoli and add the water.

Season to taste with sea salt and freshly ground black pepper.

Serve garnished with slivers of Parmesan.

Per serving: kcals 331
Carbs 41g Fat 10g Protein 16g

Oaty Chickpea Crumble

I really like the texture and flavour of chickpeas, but you could use black-eyed beans or borlotti beans instead. Oats are such a good ingredient to use and it is nice to have something savoury with them. Adding seeds to the topping increases the protein content and adds more deliciousness. I'm thinking that chopped hazelnuts would be particularly good next time... Of course, you can vary the vegetables according to the season and it is quite a useful way of using up small quantities, which may be lurking in the bottom of the fridge.

Serves 4

> **1 tsp sunflower oil 40 kcals**
>
> **A little vegetable stock or water**
>
> **1/2 onion, peeled and chopped 23 kcals**
>
> **1 medium leek, sliced 56 kcals**
>
> **1 clove garlic, peeled and crushed 4 kcals**
>
> **1 stick celery, chopped 8 kcals**
>
> **1/2 sweet red pepper, chopped 20 kcals**
>
> **2 carrots, peeled and grated 52 kcals**

200g canned chickpeas, drained and rinsed 138 kcals

1/4 tsp cumin seeds

1/4 tsp ground cumin

1/4 tsp ground cinnamon

1 tbsp tomato paste 4 kcals

2 peeled plum tomatoes (fresh or canned) 56 kcals

1 tbsp coriander leaves, finely chopped

1 tbsp Tamari soy sauce

150ml water

Freshly ground black pepper

For the crumble topping:

75g porridge oats 282 kcals

25g unsalted butter 180 kcals

10g sunflower, pumpkin or sesame seeds, or a mixture 60 kcals

Pre-heat the oven to 180c (fan).

Stir-fry the onion, garlic, celery and pepper in the oil over medium heat, for about 8 minutes, until the vegetables begin to soften.

Add the grated carrots, tomato paste, tomatoes, chickpeas and spices together with 150ml water and simmer for 10 - 15 minutes. Season with soy sauce and pepper to taste and stir in the coriander.

Meanwhile, make the topping with the oats and butter, rubbing together to make a nice crumbly mixture.

Divide the chickpeas between 4 individual ovenproof dishes, or one large one. Distribute the crumble mix over the top and sprinkle with seeds.

Bake in the oven for 25 - 30 minutes, until the top is golden.

Per serving: kcals 232
Carbs 31g Fat 10g Protein 8g

Serve with **Pepper, Chilli and Mango Salsa** (page 124) and **Broccoli and Tofu Stir-Fry** (this page).

Broccoli, Green Bean and Tofu Stir Fry

This is an interesting side dish to serve with Oaty Chickpea Crumble, or as part of a vegetarian meal.

Serves 2

1 tsp sunflower oil 40 kcals

1 onion, sliced 46 kcals

1 clove garlic, finely chopped 4 kcals

100g broccoli florets 34 kcals

100g green beans, trimmed 32 kcals

100g pressed tofu 70 kcals

1/2 tbsp Tamari soy sauce 6 kcals

1 tsp root ginger, finely chopped 2 kcals

Drain the tofu and pat dry with kitchen paper, then cut the tofu into small squares, toss in the soy sauce and set aside.

Heat the oil in a wok over medium heat and stir-fry the onions, garlic and ginger adding a little water as necessary, until the onions have softened.

Add the broccoli and beans and steam-fry for a further 3 or 4 minutes, so the vegetables still have some bite to them.

Stir in the tofu with the soy sauce and heat through.

Serve immediately.

You could garnish with finely chopped coriander leaf, or add some toasted sesame or sunflower seeds.

Per Serving: kcals 115
Carbs 14g Fat 5g Protein 8g

Steam-fried Swiss Chard with Bean Sprouts and Mushrooms

It's something of a treat for me to have bean sprouts, as they are not available in our local shops, but if I go to the market in Montaigu de Quercy on a Saturday, there is a stall there that specialises in them. I could happily eat this all on its own, but it also makes a great base for **Tuna Steak Marinaded in Ginger and Garlic** (page 89).

Serves 2 as a side dish

> 1 tsp sunflower oil 42 kcals
>
> A little water
>
> 1/2 onion, finely sliced 22 kcals
>
> 1/2 leek, cleaned and finely sliced 28 kcals
>
> 200g beanshoots 58 kcals
>
> 100g mushrooms, cleaned and sliced 22 kcals
>
> 200g Swiss chard, chopped, green and stems separated 38 kcals

Heat the oil in a wok or frying pan and add the onion and leek, stir-frying over medium heat until they are softened. Add a little water together with the mushrooms and steam-fry* for a few minutes, until the mushrooms are starting to release their moisture, then add the Swiss chard stems. Give them a couple of minutes before adding the green leaves. They need to be wilted but still bright green when you add the bean sprouts, which you need to cook for just long enough for them to heat through.

Serve immediately.

Per serving: kcals 104
Carbs 15g Fat 3g Protein 8g

As a vegetarian main dish, serve with a little Tamari soy sauce or a tahini dressing, together with some toasted almonds or smoked tofu and a portion of brown rice or **Cauliflower Rice** (page 84).

Fragrant Tofu and Vegetables with Brown Rice

This dish has a lovely variety of textures. The addition of some Thai green curry paste and light coconut milk makes a tasty sauce. Try and keep your portions of starchy carbs to be no bigger than your fist. Wholegrain brown rice is a healthier choice than white rice, with more fibre and nutrients and a lower GI. I have used purple mange tout, runner beans and oyster mushrooms, but you can vary these according to what is in season - bearing in mind that mushrooms are very low in calorie, so a great way of bulking up a dish without making it fattening.

Serves 2

> 50g wholegrain basmati rice 168 kcals
>
> 100g tofu 166 kcals
>
> 125ml light coconut milk 164 kcals
>
> 1 tbsp Thai green curry paste 16 kcals
>
> 50g purple or green mange tout 14 kcals
>
> 50g fine green beans 14 kcals
>
> 100g oyster mushrooms, cleaned 43 kcals

Weigh out the rice in a cup (if you have add-and-weigh scales) or weigh and then transfer to a cup, so that you can tell how much volume it has.

Wash the rice in a sieve, then add to a saucepan with twice its volume of cold water.

Bring to the boil, add a little salt if you wish, then cover with a lid and turn to the lowest possible heat.

Leave to cook for about 20 minutes, until all the water is absorbed and the grains are tender (different varieties of rice can take different times to cook).

Meanwhile, cut the tofu into cubes and pat dry on kitchen paper.

Put a wok or frying pan over medium heat and pour in the coconut milk.

Add the curry paste, mix in well and bring to a simmer.

Add the vegetables and tofu, put on a lid and allow to cook for 3 or 4 minutes so that the beans and mange-tout still have a bit of crunch.

This technique, of making a fragrant and spicy coconut sauce to cook in, also works very well with firm white fish or chicken.

Per serving: kcals 292
Carbs 28g Fat 14g Protein 16g

Leek and Crunchy Carrot Gratin

This is a very flavourful vegetarian main which is low enough in calories to have on a 5:2 Fast Day or as part of a calorie-counted healthy eating plan. It would also work well to serve as a side dish with sausages (baked in the oven at the same time)

With the vegetables, milk, cheese, breadcrumbs and nuts, this has a good balance of ingredients. I used oddments of cheese that I had left - a little cheddar, some Comté and some crumbled blue sheep's cheese, which worked fine, but you can use any hard cheese really. The caraway seeds add a really interesting flavour.

Serves 5

500g leeks, cut into chunks 155 kcals
150ml vegetable stock or water 12 kcals
1 tsp caraway seeds 7 kcals
250ml semi-skimmed milk 113 kcals
10g unsalted butter 70 kcals
1 tbsp plain flour 52 kcals
Sea salt and freshly ground black pepper to taste

For the topping
60g fresh wholewheat breadcrumbs 127 kcals
2 medium carrots, grated 50 kcals
75g grated hard cheese 312 kcals
15g chopped walnuts 98 kcals

Preheat the oven to 180c (fan).

Put the leeks in a saucepan with the stock or water and seeds.

Bring to the boil, cover and then simmer for 7 to 10 minutes, until the leeks are softened.

Remove the leeks with a slotted draining spoon and transfer to a baking dish.

Pour the remaining liquid into a jug and make up to 300ml with milk.

Melt the butter in a saucepan over medium-low heat.

When it starts to froth, add the flour and mix well with a wooden spoon to make a roux.

Remove from the heat and gradually add the liquid, beating well after each addition, to make a smooth sauce.

Return to the heat and simmer the sauce for a couple of minutes, stirring all the time, to make sure that it doesn't burn and there are no lumps.

Check the seasoning.

Pour over the leeks.

Mix all the topping ingredients together and sprinkle over the top.

Bake in the oven for 20 - 25 minutes, until golden.

Serve with some fresh green vegetables, such as steamed broccoli.

Per serving: kcals 199
Carbs 20g Fat 10g Protein 7g

Jerusalem Artichoke and Goat's Cheese Gratin

This is totally delicious and has lovely textures. This makes a great feature of Jerusalem Artichokes.

Serves 3

- **450 grams Jerusalem artichokes 328 kcals**
- **40g shelled walnut pieces 250 kcals**
- **1/2 tbsp olive oil 60 kcals**
- **A pinch of nutmeg, freshly grated**
- **Freshly ground black pepper**
- **100ml water**
- **3 small leeks 162 kcals**
- **56g (2 Cabécou) soft goats' cheese 154 kcals**
- **A couple of sprigs of fresh thyme**

Heat oven to 200c (fan)

Peel or scrub the artichokes, keeping them under water to stop them going brown.

Slice the artichokes into rounds, about 5mm (1/4") thick.

Cook in boiling lightly salted water for about 3 minutes, until slightly soft, then drain.

Toast the walnuts in a dry frying pan until slightly coloured, then chop finely.

Trim, wash and slice the leeks finely.

Heat the oil in a saucepan, add the leeks, nutmeg and pepper, stir-fry for a minute or two, then add about 100ml of water.

Put a lid on, lower the heat to minimum and cook for about 10 minutes until soft and luscious, adding a little more water if needed.

Transfer the leeks to an ovenproof dish, then layer the artichokes on top.

Distribute the nuts and then crumble the goats' cheese on top.

Strip the thyme leaves from the stalks and sprinkle over.

Bake in the oven for 20 – 25 minutes, until the cheese is starting to brown.

Per serving: kcals 314
Carbs 40g Fat 15g Protein 10g

Serve with a **Rocket and Orange Salad** (page 47), dressed with squeezed orange juice and a few drops of aged balsamic vinegar.

Pommes Dauphinoise ~ Dauphinoise Potatoes

There must be as many variations of this dish as there are varieties of potatoes... I have used Raymond Blanc's method, from his book *"Simple French Cookery"* - I like it because the potatoes are pre-cooked in the milk and cream, ensuring that they will be soft and luscious after a much shorter cooking time in the oven than most other recipes. This is an absolute winner with **Beef and Carrot Casserole** (page 102).

Serves 4

- **400g firm red potatoes, washed 280 kcals**
- **200ml semi-skimmed milk 99 kcals**
- **50ml full fat cream 175 kcals**
- **1 clove garlic, peeled and halved 4 kcals**
- **Sea salt and freshly ground black pepper**
- **1/2 tsp freshly ground nutmeg 6 kcals**
- **50g grated Emmental cheese 214 kcals**

Preheat the oven to 160c (fan).

Peel and slice the potatoes finely, but don't rinse them or pat them dry, as the starch is an important factor for the consistency of the final dish.

Put the milk and cream into a saucepan and bring to the boil over medium heat.

Meanwhile rub an ovenproof dish all over with the garlic, then finely slice up what remains.

Add the potato slices and mix well to coat in the mixture.

Add the finely sliced garlic (if you like a good flavour of it, as we do!).

Season with salt and pepper and a good grating of nutmeg.

Lower the heat and simmer for 8 minutes, stirring every so often to ensure that the potatoes don't stick to the bottom of the pan.

Remove the pan from the heat and stir in the cheese.

Transfer to the ovenproof dish and level the top.

Bake in the oven for 30 - 40 minutes, until the top is golden brown.

Per serving: kcals 195
Carbs 19g Fat 10g Protein 7g

Tian of Vegetables with Mozzarella

A Tian is a dish of baked chopped vegetables named after a traditional earthenware cooking pot used in Provence in the South of France. The mozzarella is added just for the last part of the cooking time.

Serves 4

1 clove garlic, peeled 4 kcals
1 aubergine, finely sliced 132 kcals
2 courgettes, finely sliced 64 kcals
1 red pepper, finely sliced 36 kcals
1 yellow pepper, finely sliced 52 kcals
2 tomatoes, finely sliced 44 kcals
Sea salt and freshly ground black pepper
1 tbsp olive oil 120 kcals
2 mozzarella, sliced 172 kcals
2 sprigs thyme 4 kcals
2 sprigs rosemary 8 kcals

Preheat oven to 200c (fan).

Cut the garlic in half and rub the inside of an ovenproof dish.

Lay the finely chopped vegetables in the dish, arranging the colours pleasingly, then season generously with pepper and a little salt.

Drizzle with a little olive oil.

Bake in the oven for about 45 minutes

Distribute the mozzarella over the vegetables, top with the herbs and bake for a further 10 minutes.

Per serving: kcals 159
Carbs 20g Fat 7g Protein 8g

Serve immediately with **Rosemary Focaccia** (page 131) and **Green Salad with Nuts and Seeds** (page 41).

Tian of Vegetables with Mozzarella

Patatas Bravas

This is a classic tapas dish from Spain that can be served alongside drinks, or works brilliantly as a side dish with **Tortilla** (page 58) or **Spanish Style Chicken with Garlic** (page 121).

Serves 2

> 200g firm potatoes, cut into small cubes 138 kcals
>
> 1 tsp olive oil 40 kcals
>
> Sea salt

For the tomato sauce

> 1 tsp olive oil 40 kcals
>
> 1 clove garlic, finely chopped 4 kcals
>
> 200g tomatoes, skinned and crushed (or passata) 36 kcals
>
> 1/2 small onion, finely chopped 14 kcals
>
> 1 tbsp tomato paste 13 kcals
>
> 1/4 tsp chilli powder
>
> 50ml white wine 41 kcals
>
> A dash of Tabasco sauce
>
> Sea salt and freshly ground black pepper

Preheat oven to 180c (fan).

Put the potato cubes in a plastic bag along with the oil and shake gently.

Layer the potatoes onto a baking sheet and sprinkle with a little salt.

Bake for about 40 minutes, until nicely browned.

Meanwhile, heat the oil in a frying and sauté the onion and garlic until softened.

Add the tomatoes and cook for 3 or 4 minutes, then stir in the tomato paste, chilli, wine and Tabasco.

Season with salt and pepper, then cover and simmer gently for about 30 minutes.

Add a little water if necessary to make a nice smooth consistency.

Serve the potatoes in the sauce, or with cocktail sticks to spear the potatoes with and the sauce in a bowl alongside to dip them into.

Per serving kcals 163
Carbs 24g Fat 5g Protein 3g

You can use potatoes cooked in this way as an interesting appetiser, by mixing some Tabasco sauce and tomato paste into some mayonnaise to serve as a dip.

Cheesy-topped Sweet Potato

I often serve sweet potatoes just as they come out of the oven, split and topped with a little butter, but this recipe calls for a little extra work, which is well worthwhile!

Serves 2

> 1 sweet potato 103 kcals
>
> 2 tsp lime juice 3 kcals
>
> 2 tsp coconut cream 23 kcals
>
> Sea salt and freshly ground black pepper
>
> 20g grated cheese 81 kcals

To garnish

> Parsley or coriander leaves
>
> Lime zest

Preheat oven to 180c (fan).

Bake the potato until just soft *(see Tip).

Remove from the oven and leave until cool enough to handle, then cut in half and carefully scoop out the flesh, reserving the skins.

Mash the flesh with the lime juice and coconut cream and season to taste.

Spoon the mixture back into the skins and top with the grated cheese.

Return to a high shelf in the oven and bake until the cheese melts.

Serve garnished with some chopped herbs and a little lime zest.

Per serving: kcals 104
Carbs 13g Fat 5g Protein 4g

Serve with **Spiced Pork Chop with Spring Onions** (page 103).

Mixed Steamed Vegetables

I have included this as an example of the quantity of vegetables you can have for relatively few calories! A great way to fill your plate with good things.

Serves 2

> 50g spinach leaves, washed and roughly torn if large 13 kcals
>
> 60g broccoli florets 20 kcals
>
> 60g carrots, peeled and cut into julienne strips 25 kcals
>
> 30g celeriac, peeled and cut into small cubes 13 kcals
>
> 40g mange tout, trimmed 13 kcals

Per serving: 42 kcals
Carbs 9g Fat 0g Protein 3g

An ideal mix to go with **Salmon Teriyaki with Leeks** (page 96), as shown.

> ### * Tip: Baking Sweet Potatoes
>
> To help sweet potatoes to cook more quickly, thread a metal skewer through them lengthwise.
>
> This helps to distribute the heat right to the centre.

A great selection at the local market

Prepared vegetables ready for steaming

In the late 70s I first started writing a cookbook, but the frustrations of writing with an old-fashioned typewriter led to that project being shelved and it took another 30 or so years before I actually got round to completing one!

Interestingly, many of my ideas have come full circle, and now I am back to the same tenets of eating local, fresh and seasonal ingredients, eating less meat and avoiding processed foods.

Nut roast or burgers

1-1½ cups chopped or ground nuts (almonds are my favourite, but hazels or
        mixed nuts are also good)
½-¾ cup wholewheat breadcrumbs (2 thick slices)
2 crumbled ryvita (optional)
1 or 2 Onions, finely chopped
1 Egg, beaten
Salt , pepper , tamari,
Milk or water to mix
Parsley

Mix dry ingredients. Fry onions until well browned. Add to mixture and mix well. Then add beaten egg. Add seasonings and then add liquid until the mixture will hold together.
For a roast, put the mixture into a lightly greased loaf tin and bake in the oven, moderately hot for 40-45 minutes. Can be frozen before or after baking. Can be eaten hot or cold. Cold slices can be frozen separately.
For rissoles, take handfuls of the mixture (wet hands are less messy) and form into balls, flatten and then coat with seasoned flour or a mixture of flour and oats, or egg and breadrrumbs. Fry for at least 5 minutes each side in shallow oil.

Variations : Add grated carrot and/or finely chopped celery to the mixture. Add leftover cooked vegetables or rice. Use nuts that are finely ground for a smooth texture, or coarsley chopped for a more crunchy mix.

Nut Loaf

The origin of this recipe is from vegetarian friends whom I shared a kitchen with in the late 70s, a time when I used to buy wholefoods in bulk from the warehouse to split and distribute among friends and neighbours, as there was no health food shop nearby. I have been making variations of it ever since.

The same mix can be used to make patties or sausage shapes, which need to be shaped with damp hands and then rolled in seasoned flour or oats before frying. You can vary the mix of nuts - almonds are a particular favourite of mine, but in early November I made the most of the new seasons' hazelnuts, walnuts and chestnuts.

Serves 6

- 1 tbsp sunflower oil 120 kcals
- 2 onions, finely chopped 90 kcals
- 1 clove garlic, crushed, 4 kcals
- 1 stalk celery, finely chopped 9 kcals
- 1/2 red chilli, deseeded and finely chopped 5 kcals
- 200g mixed shelled nuts
- 100g shelled walnuts 654 kcals
- 50g peeled chestnuts 123 kcals
- 50g shelled hazelnuts 314 kcals
- 2 tbsp finely chopped parsley 2 kcal
- 2 rye crisp-bread, crumbled 70 kcals
- 50g wholewheat bread (without crust) 106 kcals
- 1 medium carrot, grated 25 kcals
- Freshly ground black pepper
- Tamari soy sauce
- 1 egg, lightly beaten 70 kcals

About 2 tbsp soya milk or vegetable stock, to bind 10 kcals

Preheat oven to 180c (fan).

Grease a loaf tin thoroughly with a little of the sunflower oil.

Heat a frying pan and add the remaining oil, then gently fry the onions, garlic, celery and chilli until they are soft and the onions are starting to brown a little at the edges.

Whizz the nuts in a food processor or use a hand chopper, to chop finely, then put into a mixing bowl.

Cut the bread into cubes and add to a food processor or blender along with the parsley and pulse to fine crumbs.

Add the breadcrumbs, crispbread, grated carrot and cooked vegetables to the nuts.

Mix in the egg with a fork and add enough liquid to bind the mixture together, then season well with pepper and Tamari.

Turn into the loaf tin and spread evenly.

Bake in the centre of the oven for 30 - 40 minutes, until nicely browned.

Turn out and serve cut into thick slices.

Per serving: kcals 268
Carbs 19g Fat 20g Protein 6g

Braised Red Cabbage with Lardons and Walnuts

I'm a recent convert to the pleasures of red cabbage and this is one of the ways of cooking it that helped the process. This goes extremely well with Roast Pork.

Serves 2

> **50g smoked bacon lardons 135 kcals**
>
> **2 cloves garlic, sliced 8 kcals**
>
> **1 shallot, sliced 7 kcals**
>
> **1/4 medium red cabbage, core removed, shredded 56 kcals**
>
> **1 tsp aged balsamic vinegar 1 kcals**
>
> **30ml red wine 25 kcals**
>
> **100 ml water**
>
> **1/2 tsp ground cinnamon 3 kcals**
>
> **15g shelled walnuts 94 kcals**

Heat a frying pan over medium heat and cook the lardons, garlic and shallots until they start to colour.

Add the cabbage and cook for a further 5 minutes.

Add the red wine and vinegar, bring to the boil, then simmer for 5 minutes.

Add the water and continue cooking until the cabbage is tender, about another 5 minutes.

Meanwhile, toast the walnuts in a dry frying pan over medium heat, until lightly coloured.

Season the cabbage to taste and serve with the walnuts on top.

Per serving: kcals 165
Carbs 10g Fat 10g Protein 8g

Skordalia ~ Garlic Creamed Potatoes

There are many variations of this dish and they range from an almost liquid dip to something that more closely resembles mashed potato. I've opted for somewhere in the middle, soft and smooth but still with some substance, so that you can eat it rather than dip into it. This is based on John Torode's recipe, but I have used a lot less olive oil, so the dish is lighter and firmer. It goes brilliantly well with the **Herb-crusted Lamb Chops** (page 104).

Serves 2

> **250g potatoes, peeled 173 kcals**
>
> **2 cloves garlic, peeled 9 kcals**
>
> **100ml milk 52 kcals**
>
> **2 tbsp olive oil 240 kcals**
>
> **Sea salt and freshly ground black pepper**
>
> **Juice of 1 lemon 17 kcals**
>
> **A handful of flat leaved parsley, finely chopped**

Put the potatoes, garlic, milk and olive oil into a heavy saucepan with a little salt, bring to the boil, then cover and simmer for 15 to 20 minutes, until the potatoes are soft.

Add the lemon juice and mash until smooth (easily done with a masher attachment on a hand blender) or transfer to a food processor and whizz until creamy.

Stir in the parsley and keep warm until ready to serve.

Per serving: 245 kcals
Carbs 26g Fat 15g Protein 4g

Summer Squash Slices

These make the most of seasonal summer ingredients and are a great way of getting pizza flavours without the dough. You can use large courgettes or patty pan squash. Serve them as a starter, a light lunch with a lovely salad, or as a side dish.

Serves 2

> **1 large courgette (250g) or 4 small patty pan (scallop) squash 40 kcals**
>
> **1 tsp olive oil 40 kcals**
>
> **1 large tomato, sliced 32 kcals**
>
> **1/2 clove garlic, peeled OR a pinch of garlic powder 2 kcals**
>
> **15g feta cheese 40 kcals**
>
> **15g grated Emmental 54 kcals**
>
> **Freshly ground black pepper**

To garnish

> **Basil leaves or mint leaves, finely sliced**

Preheat the oven to 210c (fan).

Cut the courgette or squashes into two halves lengthwise and trim a little off the bottom, so that they will sit well.

Lay them on a non-stick baking tray and brush lightly with olive oil.

Rub the surface with the cut clove of garlic, or sprinkle with garlic powder.

Top each half with a slice of tomato and some pieces of feta cheese or with grated Emmental with a slice of tomato on top.

Scatter chopped mint or basil over the top and season well with pepper.

Drizzle over any remaining oil.

Bake near the top of the oven for about 15 minutes, until melted and golden.

There are lots of other ideas that you could use as toppings - olives, sliced artichoke hearts, pine nuts, capers, or anchovies, tuna, salami or chorizo for the non-veggies.

Per serving: kcals 104
Carbs 8g Fat 7g Protein 6g

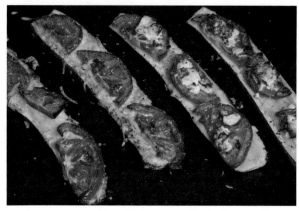

Cauliflower Rice

This provides a great low-calorie alternative to rice go with main dishes on a fast day. You can have it plain as a substitute for steamed or boiled rice, or you can treat it like a pilaf.

To make the cauliflower 'rice', cut cauliflower into florets and then pulse in a food processor until it resembles coarse grains, or grate it. The raw cauliflower grains can be frozen.

To cook, either dry fry in a non-stick pan for a few minutes or microwave for 1 - 2 minutes. Don't be tempted to add any water.

As the cauliflower doesn't absorb water in the way that rice does, the quantity you cook will be the quantity you have to put on the plate.

Cauliflower Mash

A legacy from our days of trying the South Beach Diet is what is known in that book as Surprise Mashed 'Potatoes'. These days I use real butter and cream instead of low-fat substitutes. It makes a very good accompaniment to many dishes on a fast day, such as **Chicken with Saffron and Garlic** (page 121).

Serves 4

450g cauliflower florets 113 kcals

10g butter 72 kcals

1 tbsp crème fraîche 26 kcals

Sea salt and freshly ground black pepper

Cut the cauliflower into florets and steam until soft. Mash with the butter and cream and season to taste.

Per serving: kcals 52
Carbs 6g fat 3g Protein 2g

Pumpkin and Celeriac Galettes

I spotted this idea in the little magazine that is given away in the local supermarket. They were called 'paillasson de légumes', which literally means vegetable doormats - somehow that doesn't sound so appealing in English!

Serves 4

350g peeled and grated celeriac 147 kcals

350g peeled and grated pumpkin 119 kcals

1 large organic egg 72 kcals

2 tbsp plain flour 57 kcals

1 tbsp olive oil 120 kcals

Sea salt and freshly ground black pepper

Put the grated vegetables in 2 separate bowls.

Beat the egg lightly with a fork and divide between the two bowls. Add a tablespoonful of flour to each bowl, season with salt and pepper and mix well.

Heat a little oil in a non-stick frying pan over medium heat. Drop large spoonfuls of the mixture into the pan and quickly flatten out with the back of the spoon. You should be able to get 4 into a pan at one time. Cook each galettes for a few minutes on each side, until golden.

Continue until all the mixture is used, adding a little more oil if needed for each batch Lift out as they are ready and keep warm on a baking sheet in the oven, at a low temperature.

Per serving: kcals 129
Carbs 18g Fat 5g Protein 4g

Delicious served with Duck.

Fish

I love fish but I hate what has been happening with the fishing industry, with discards, over-fishing and a general failure to treasure the wonderful resources that the sea provides.

We all have a responsibility for eating only sustainable species and for encouraging the use of ethical and environmentally friendly fishing methods.

My husband is not a fan of getting bones in his mouth when eating, nor of fiddling about with his food trying to avoid them and I'm allergic to shellfish.

We live about as far from the sea as you can get in France, so there's not much in the way of a local catch or inshore fishing fleet to support.

So all in all, I'm left with few choices when it comes to fish.... it usually comes down to anchovies, farmed salmon and trout, haddock, cod, mackerel, sardines, tuna, red mullet and some flat fish like lemon sole.

See the Marine Conservation Society web site for information on sustainable species: you can download an app and a pocket guide.

Sole with Lemon and Caper Dressing

The caper dressing adds a little zing without overpowering the light and delicately flavoured fish.

Serves 2

> 2 lemon sole (100g - 130g each) or other flat white fish 205 kcals
>
> 10g unsalted butter 72 kcals
>
> 4g capers, drained and chopped
>
> 2 tbsp flat leaved parsley, finely chopped
>
> 1 clove garlic, crushed 4 kcals
>
> Juice of a lemon 12 kcals
>
> 1 tbsp plain flour 28 kcals
>
> Sea salt and freshly ground black pepper

Skin the fish and trim as wished. Dust the fish in seasoned flour.

Melt the butter in a non-stick frying pan until frothy. Fry the fish for 2 to 3 minutes on each side, until cooked through.

Remove the fish to hot serving plates and keep warm.

Add lemon juice to deglaze the pan, then add the garlic, parsley and capers. Season to taste with salt and pepper and cook for a couple of minutes.

Pour over the fish and serve with a pleasing array of vegetables and a wedge of lemon.

Per serving: kcals 160
Carbs 4g fat 5g Protein 22g

With vegetables as shown :-

> 180g cauliflower 45 kcals
>
> 110 g asparagus 22 kcals
>
> 60g flat beans 10 kcals
>
> 75g carrots 31 kcals

Per serving: kcals 214
Carbs 16g Fat 5g Protein 26g

Peppered Mackerel with Horseradish Dressing

I buy the peppered mackerel ready prepared; it helps to raise our intake of good oily fish and makes an easy lunch or supper dish.

Serves 2

> 150g smoked peppered mackerel fillets 390 kcals
>
> 75g natural yogurt 55 kcals
>
> 2 tsp horseradish 20 kcals
>
> 2 tsp lemon juice 3 kcals

Remove the skin from the mackerel and check for and remove any bones.

Mix the yogurt with the horseradish and lemon juice to make a smooth and creamy dressing.

Per serving: kcals 234
Carbs 2g Fat 16g Protein 18g

Excellent served with **Fennel and Citrus Salad** (page 49) and **Piquant Beetroot Relish** (page 125).

Tuna Marinaded in Ginger and Garlic

Tuna has a wonderful texture and can stand up well to robust flavours. This can be made with fresh or frozen fish.

Serves 2

> **2 tuna steaks, each 100g 216 kcals**

For the marinade

> **1 tbsp Tamari soy sauce 15 kcals**
>
> **25g hoisin sauce 58 kcals**
>
> **2.5 cm piece ginger root, finely chopped 2 kcals**
>
> **1 clove garlic, finely chopped 4kcals**
>
> **1/2 tsp cumin seeds, crushed**
>
> **1/2 tsp coriander seeds, crushed**

For garnish

> **1 tbsp flat leaf parsley, finely chopped**
>
> **A squeeze of lime juice**

Mix the marinade ingredients together and pour over the fish.

Leave to marinade for at least 30 minutes.

Heat a non-stick frying pan over medium heat and put the fish steaks in, reserving the marinade.

Cook the fish for 2-3 minutes on each side, until just cooked through.

Keep warm while you finish the sauce.

Add the reserved marinade to the pan and stir-fry to cook the ginger and garlic.

Add a little water if necessary to make a smooth sauce.

Serve the fish on top of a pile of vegetables, spoon the sauce over the top and garnish with parsley and a squeeze of lime juice.

Per serving: kcals 148
Carbs 8g Fat 1g Protein 25g

Anchovies with Capers and Pine Nuts

We visited one of the villages of the Cinque Terre, in Northern Italy - a world heritage site. The 5 villages are inaccessible by car, but can be reached by the coastal train service, or by boat. Sitting by the harbour at Vernazza, I chose this as my first course and it has been a favourite to serve as an appetiser or starter ever since.

You can usually find ready-marinaded anchovies in the chiller cabinet of large supermarkets.

Capers come in various sizes, from the tiny 'nonpareil' to the large caperberries - they all have the necessary bitterness that provides the contrast to the luscious oil, sharp citrus and almost sweet fish.

Serves 3

> **150g white anchovies, marinaded in garlic and oil 203 kcals**
>
> **25g pine nuts, toasted 146 kcals**
>
> **30g (1 heaped tbsp) capers, drained 7 kcals**
>
> **Zest of 1 lemon, slivered**
>
> **1 tbsp extra virgin olive oil 120 kcals**

Toast the pine nuts in a dry frying pan until starting to turn golden brown. Leave to cool.

Remove the anchovies from the marinade and arrange on a serving dish.

Drizzle the olive oil over the fish and scatter the capers, lemon zest and pine nuts.

This could be an occasion for having some soft bread, as you will really want to mop up the gorgeous oil....

Per serving: kcals 160
Carbs 2g Fat 13g Protein 11g

Thai Salmon Patties with Pickled Vegetable Ribbons

I had always thought that fish cakes needed potato or something to hold them together, but not so, these work beautifully. I like to make them small so that they cook quickly and the centre stays moist and pink. The recipe was based on one in the BBC Good Food site's healthy collection.

Serves 2

> 250g salmon fillets 244 kcals
>
> 2 tsp grated root ginger 4 kcals
>
> 1 tbsp chopped coriander leaf
>
> 1 tsp Thai red curry paste 10 kcals
>
> 1 tbsp Tamari soy sauce 16 kcals
>
> 1 tsp maple syrup 12 kcals
>
> 1/2 tbsp rice wine vinegar 6 kcals
>
> 1 carrot 26 kcals
>
> 1/2 cucumber 18 kcals
>
> 2 spring onions 10 kcals
>
> 1 tbsp sunflower oil 120 kcals

Put the salmon, ginger, coriander, Thai curry paste and Tamari into a food processor and whizz until the fish is minced. With damp hands, form into 6 patties. Keep them cool while you prepare the vegetables.

Mix the vinegar and maple syrup in a bowl.

Peel the carrot and cucumber into long strips or ribbons and cut the spring onion into long slivers. Add to the bowl and toss together well.

Heat the oil in a frying pan over medium heat and fry the patties for a couple of minutes on each side, until just cooked through.

Serve immediately with the vegetable pickle.

For a main meal, also serve some steamed broccoli and wilted spinach.

Per serving: kcals 228
Carbs 12g Fat 11g 7g

Cod and Chips with Salsa Brava

The idea of fish and chips has a strong hold on the British imagination, but I have to say that this was probably even more delicious than having the fish swathed in batter, which is so often greasy and disappointingly soggy. Here I have paired a nice piece of cod with a Spanish style salsa brava with a little chorizo, which set it off beautifully. If you want a quicker method of making the sauce, use canned chopped tomatoes, which won't require the extra simmering time.

Serves 4

> 4 thick cod fillets, about 100g each 392 kcals
>
> A little olive oil 40 kcals
>
> 1/2 tsp smoked paprika 4 kcals
>
> Sea salt and freshly ground black pepper
>
> 400g frozen oven chips* 552 kcals

For the salsa brava (can be made ahead)

> 1 tsp olive oil 40 kcals
>
> 1/2 onion, finely chopped 22 kcals
>
> 1 clove garlic 4 kcals
>
> 50g chorizo 228 kcals
>
> 400g tomatoes, peeled and chopped 72 kcals

1 tbsp tomato paste 14 kcals

A pinch chilli powder or flakes 2 kcals

A dash of Tabasco sauce

Sea salt and freshly ground black pepper

A little water

Preheat the oven to 200c (fan).

Heat the olive oil in a frying pan and gently sauté the onions and garlic together with the chorizo until the vegetables are softened.

Add the tomatoes, tomato paste, chilli and Tabasco and season to taste.

Cover and simmer for about 20 minutes, adding water as necessary to keep it to a nice saucy texture.

Put the frozen chips onto a baking tray and cook in the oven for 15 minutes, or according to packet directions.

Meanwhile, preheat the grill to high (or put a pan of water on if you prefer to steam the fish).

Brush the fish with olive oil and sprinkle with the paprika and season with salt and pepper.

Grill or steam the fish for 5 to 6 minutes, until cooked through.

Serve with the salsa brava and chips. Steamed green beans make the perfect accompaniment (27 kcals per 100g).

*Instead of using oven chips you can make your own baked potato wedges - wash and cut 500g firm potatoes into wedges, no need to peel. Put on a non-stick baking tray. Brush lightly with olive oil, sprinkle with salt and pepper and bake for about 30 minutes until golden at 200c (fan), shaking the tray occasionally to ensure even browning. These will be lower in calories than ready-made ones, plus you get the benefit of the vitamins under the skin of the potatoes. These can be sprinkled with herbs or spices before baking, if you wish.

Per serving: kcals 342
Carbs 35g Fat 12g Protein 24g

Any leftover salsa brava can frozen and later be used to go with dishes such as **Baked Salmon with a Light Caper Dressing** (page 98) or **Patatas Bravas** (page 78).

Herring with Beetroot and an Avocado Salad

I'm not a great fan of herring because of all the small bones, but it does have a fine flavour. I found that by cutting it into small strips I was able to create some nice mini fillets - and no bones. A strong mustardy dressing made with a little olive oil, Dijon mustard and some lemon juice suits it well and I served it with garlic mash, some sliced beetroot and an avocado salad.

Serves 1

1 smoked herring 100 kcals

1 cup mixed salad (rocket, radish, celery, onion, grated carrot) 24 kcals

1/4 avocado, chopped 98 kcals

1 tbsp mustard vinaigrette 41 kcals

1 beetroot, sliced 44 kcals

100g Garlic Creamed Potatoes (page 82) 113 kcals

Per serving: kcals 421
Carbs 28g Fat 28g Protein 14g

You could reduce the calories by using **Cauliflower Mash** (page 84).

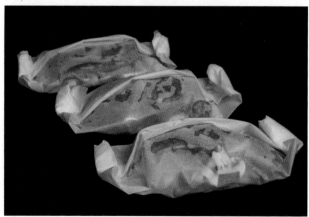

This way of wrapping fish and baking in the oven conserves all the moisture

Salmon Stuffed with Pine Nuts and Herbs

This is a splendid idea that came from Annabel Langbein's book *"Cooking to Impress without Stress"*.

Serves 4

> **4 salmon fillets (each about 150g), skinned 846 kcals**
>
> **Finely grated zest and juice of 1 lemon 14 kcals**
>
> **1 bunch flat leaved parsley, finely chopped 4 kcals**
>
> **1 tsp capers, roughly chopped**
>
> **2 tbsp pine nuts or chopped walnuts 114 kcals**
>
> **sea salt and freshly ground black pepper**

To serve
> **6 lemon wedges 14 kcals**

Heat the oven to 220°C (fan)

Lay the fish onto a non-stick baking sheet.

Cut a diagonal slash in the top of each one.

Mix the parsley, nuts, capers and lemon zest together and stuff some into each piece of fish.

Season with salt and freshly ground black pepper and squeeze lemon juice over.

Bake for 6 – 8 minutes.

Serve with a wedge or two of lemon to squeeze over.

Per serving: kcals 186
Carbs 3g Fat 11g Protein 33g

I like to present this with a rainbow of steamed and fresh vegetables - steamed multi-coloured carrots, wilted spinach, baked mushrooms, steamed asparagus and fresh tomatoes.

For a non-fast day you could add a hollandaise sauce.

Masala Baked Haddock

I came across this idea when watching Rick Stein's *Far Eastern Odyssey*. The first time I tried it I found it far too mustardy and bitter, but the idea of coating a piece of white fish with a masala paste and topping it with onions, then wrapping it in foil or baking paper to cook in the oven won me over. So I have now adapted it and am much happier with the result.

You can make the masala paste in a blender or you can pound it in a pestle and mortar.

This will be good with any firm white fish.

Serves 2

> **250g haddock or cod fillets 200 kcals**
> **1/2 red onion, finely sliced**
> **Some red or green chilli, sliced (optional)**

For the Masala

> **1 tsp black mustard seeds 16 kcals**
> **1/2 tsp cumin seeds 4 kcals**
> **1/2 tsp coriander seeds**
> **1/4 tsp chilli powder 2 kcals**
> **2 tsp sunflower oil 80 kcals**
> **1/2 onion, sliced 22 kcals**
> **1/2 tsp ground turmeric 4 kcals**
> **1 clove garlic, crushed 4 kcals**
> **1/2 tsp sea salt**

Preheat the oven to 180c (fan)

Heat the oil in a frying pan and gently fry all the masala ingredients until the onions soften and start to colour, adding a splash of water if needed to stop it sticking.

Blend into a paste, using a food processor or pestle and mortar.

Put the fish in the centre of a piece of foil or baking paper and smother with the paste.

Top with some slices of red onion and maybe a few slices of red or green chilli.

Wrap the parcels and fold over the edges securely.

Bake in the oven for about 20 minutes depending on the thickness of the fillets, until just cooked through.

Per serving: kcals 162
Carbs 4g Fat 5g Protein 24g

Serve with **Kachumber Salad** (page 49), steamed carrots and brown rice or **Cauliflower Rice** (page 84).

Salmon Baked with Pesto

Here's a simple way to give a different flavour to a salmon fillet. You can use fresh or defrosted fish for this.

Serves 1

> **100g salmon fillet, 108 kcals**
> **1 tsp pesto 28 kcals**

Preheat the oven to 180c (fan).

Put the salmon on a square of baking paper. Spread the pesto over the top. Wrap into a parcel, folding the edges together, then put onto a baking tray. Bake in the oven for about 20 minutes, until cooked through.

Here served with **Bayonne-wrapped Pumpkin** (page 71) and an assortment of steamed vegetables.

Per serving: kcals 136
Carbs 0g Fat 10g Protein 13g

Spiced Red Mullet with Coconut-Lime Sauce and Lentil Salad

I love these little fish, which have such pretty pink skin and a lovely flavour and texture. I usually buy them frozen and defrost before using.

This is a good recipe for entertaining, as the **Puy Lentil Salad** can be prepared ahead of time and the fish are quick to cook. A lower-calorie version of a BBC Good Food recipe.

Serves 4

For the red mullet

> **2 tbsp plain flour 56 kcals**
>
> **2 tsp curry powder 12 kcals**
>
> **500g red mullet fillets 544 kcals**
>
> **1 tbsp olive oil 120 kcals**

For the coconut sauce

> **20g golden raisins 60 kcals**
>
> **1/2 tsp curry powder 4 kcals**
>
> **1/2 tsp turmeric 4 kcals**
>
> **1/2 tsp ground coriander**
>
> **1/2 tsp ground cumin 4 kcals**
>
> **200ml light coconut milk 202 kcals**
>
> **Zest of 1 lime**

To serve

> **1 batch of Puy Lentil Salad** (page 50)

Check that there are no scales on the red mullet and pat dry if they have been defrosted.

Mix the spices with the flour in a shallow dish and dredge the fish in it.

Heat the olive oil in a frying pan over medium heat and cook the fillets skin side down, for a couple of minutes only, until the skin is crisp. Turn over and cook for a further minute or two, then remove once cooked through.

Increase the heat a little and add the spices and raisins to the pan, mixing in with any pan juices. Pour in the coconut milk and cook for a couple of minutes until slightly reduced.

To serve: Pile the lentil salad on individual plates and lay the fish over the top. Decorate with the sauce and sprinkle with the lime zest.

Per serving: kcals 351 (including salad) Carbs 24g Fat 19g Protein 29g

For a wheat free dish, use gram flour or maize meal for the coating.

Upside Down Fish Pie with Gremolata

This recipe has evolved from a recipe that I spotted in "delicious" magazine, where the potatoes are on the bottom and there are breadcrumbs sprinkled on the top. I particularly like it with salmon, but it works brilliantly with cod, haddock or for a real treat try it with sea bass.

Serves 4

500g red skinned potatoes, peeled and thinly sliced 352 kcals

1 red onion, thinly sliced 44 kcals

2 tsp olive oil 80 kcals

100g cherry tomatoes, halved 16 kcals

25g sundried tomatoes, sliced 64 kcals

4 fish fillets 844 kcals

1 red chilli, seeds removed, finely sliced 4 kcals

8 slices of lemon 16 kcals

60g wholewheat breadcrumbs 144 kcals

1 tbsp olive oil 120 kcals

For the Gremolata

6 marinaded anchovy fillets, chopped 24 kcals

2 cloves garlic, chopped 8 kcals

1 tbsp olive oil 120 kcals

Zest of 1 lemon

A bunch of parsley leaves, chopped 4 kcals

Preheat the oven to 180c (fan).

Brush a roasting tin with oil, then add the potatoes, onions into a roasting tray, drizzle with the remaining oil, season with salt and pepper and then mix together.

Bake for 15 minutes.

Add the tomatoes and dried tomatoes and cook for a further 15 minutes, by which time the potatoes should be nearly cooked through.

Mix the breadcrumbs with the olive oil in a plastic bag and shake to mix.

Put the fish fillets on top, decorate with lemon and chilli slices and sprinkle the breadcrumb mixture over the top.

Bake for a further 15 minutes, or until the fish is cooked through.

Meanwhile, make the Gremolata by whizzing all the ingredients in a food processor to make a sauce

Serve with the Gremolata drizzled over.

Per serving: kcals 460
Carbs 51g Fat 21g Protein 20g

If you have started the meal with a salad or a vegetable dish, there is no need to serve anything else with this, but a crisp green salad, some wilted spinach or steamed broccoli make a good visual contrast.

Salmon Teriyaki with Leeks

This Salmon dish is baked in the oven on a bed of shredded leeks, mushrooms and tomatoes and wrapped in baking parchment, which means you don't need to use any additional fat - and it cuts down on the calories. Ideal for a fast day dinner, served with some steamed vegetables.

Serves 2

1 leek, washed, trimmed and finely sliced 54 kcals

2 salmon fillets (100g each), skinned 284 kcals

1 tbsp Light Teriyaki Sauce (page 124) 20 kcals

1/2 tsp ground cumin 4 kcals

1/2 tsp ground coriander

2 slices of lime, halved 4 kcals

2 mushrooms, sliced 8 kcals

8 cherry tomatoes, halved 14 kcals

A little chopped coriander leaf or parsley 2 kcals

Heat oven to 180c (fan).

Divide the leeks, mushrooms and tomatoes between two pieces of baking parchment, placing them in the centre.

Lay the salmon on top, spoon over the teriyaki sauce and sprinkle with spices.

Top with the slices of lime.

Bake for 20 minutes.

Unwrap and sprinkle with fresh herbs.

Serve with a nice heap of Mixed Steamed Vegetables (e.g. broccoli, carrots, spinach, celeriac, mange tout).

This method of cooking fish will work with fillets of fresh or frozen firm white fish too.

Per serving: kcals 195
Carbs 12g Fat 7g Protein 22g

Haddock in Saffron Sauce

If you like the Spanish flavours of saffron and garlic, I'm sure you will enjoy this easy way of cooking fish.

This recipe is based on one in *"Tapas, the little dishes of Spain"* by Penelope Casas, where she used Swordfish or Shark – but the latter is certainly off the list of acceptable fish to use these days. I used Haddock, but it would be equally good with Cod or Halibut or a firm meaty fish like Tuna (as long as it was caught by pole and line). If you want more information about which fish are ok to eat and which aren't, please download "Fish to Eat and Fish to Avoid" or See the Marine Conservation Society web site

The lovely golden colour of the finished dish is not entirely due to saffron – the tomato I used was a heritage variety called Amish Gold.

Serves 2

240g haddock fillet, cut into cubes 268 kcals

2 tsp extra virgin olive oil 80 kcals

1/2 small onion, finely chopped 14 kcals

1 clove garlic, finely chopped or crushed 4 kcals

1/2 green pepper, finely chopped 12 kcals

250ml chicken stock 10 kcals

100g tomato, skinned and chopped 18 kcals

A pinch of saffron strands

A pinch of freshly grated nutmeg 2 kcals

Sea salt and freshly ground black pepper

Heat the oil in a frying pan or cazuela (earthenware dish).

Sauté the onions, garlic and green pepper until softened.

Add the tomato and cook for a couple of minutes.

Stir in the stock, saffron, nutmeg and season to taste.

Add the fish pieces, cover and cook for 5 to 10 minutes until the fish is cooked through.

Per serving: kcals 205
Carbs 6g Fat 6g Protein 30g

I served this with **Cauliflower Rice** (page 84) and Broad Beans.

A very satisfying and delicious main course for less than 300 kcals.

Baked Salmon with Light Caper Dressing

Another variation of the ubiquitous salmon, that regularly turns up on our plates on a fast day. I like to ring the changes, so here is baked on a bed of mushrooms and garlic and served with a light tartare-style sauce.

Serves 2

> 2 salmon fillets, 100g each, skinned 282 kcal
>
> 2 tsp olive oil, 80 kcals
>
> 100g mushrooms, cleaned and sliced 22 kcals
>
> 1 clove garlic, finely chopped 4 kcals
>
> 1 tbsp fresh parsley, finely chopped 2 kcals
>
> Sea salt and freshly ground black pepper
>
> 2 slices of lemon, halved 4 kcals

For the Caper Dressing

> 125g natural yogurt 88 kcals
>
> 2 tsp mayonnaise 70 kcals
>
> 2 tsp lemon juice 2 kcals
>
> 4 tsp capers, drained and chopped 2 kcal
>
> 10g cornichons (small gherkins), finely chopped 2 kcals

Preheat the oven to 180c (fan).

Lay out a sheet of baking paper or foil for each piece of fish, large enough to wrap it up in.

Divide the mushrooms between them, placing them in the centre, with the garlic.

Lay the fish on top, season and sprinkle with parsley.

Put the lemon slices on top, then wrap the fish up, sealing the parcels well.

Place on a baking tray and cook in the oven for about 20 minutes, until the fish is cooked through.

Meanwhile, mix together the ingredients for the dressing.

Serve the fish with the dressing alongside.

Per serving: kcals 228
Carbs 9g Fat 14g Protein 26g

Good with the addition of some **Salsa Brava** (page 90) and a generous portion of various steamed vegetables.

Avocado Rounds with Smoked Salmon

Combine some favourite ingredients to make an attractive starter or light meal. The challenge here seems to be getting the avocados at just the right consistency. I usually buy them when they are still quite firm and find that after about 3 days in the vegetable rack, they are just right. If they get a little too ripe, I use them for making **Guacamole** (page 28).

> 1 small Hass avocado 130 kcals
>
> 15g smoked trout or salmon 29 kcals
>
> 30g rocket 8 kcals
>
> 1 spring onion 5 kcals
>
> 2 baby plum tomatoes 36 kcals
>
> 1/4 lemon 6 kcals

Peel the avocado and slice across, working around the stone.

Divide the smoked trout into pieces and fold into the centre of the avocado slices.

Serve with a tangy rocket salad and serve with the lemon to squeeze over.

Per serving: kcals 213
Carbs 16g Fat 14g Protein 8g

A dab of mayonnaise under each piece of smoked fish makes a good addition.

Lemony Tuna Kebabs

Here's one for the summer BBQ.

Serves 2

  2 tuna steaks 312 kcals

  1 medium courgette, sliced 32 kcals

  1 red pepper, deseeded 36 kcals

  1 red onion, peeled 44 kcals

For the marinade

  1 tbsp olive oil 120 kcals

  1 onion, chopped 44 kcals

  2 cloves garlic, chopped 8 kcals

  Juice of 1 lemon 12 kcals

  1/2 tsp dry roasted cumin seeds, crushed 4 kcals

  1/2 tsp dry roasted coriander seeds, crushed 2 kcals

  A handful of fresh herbs - parsley, coriander, thyme, marjoram or basil

  Sea salt and freshly ground black pepper

Whizz all the marinade ingredients in a good processor to make a fairly smooth paste.

Cut the tuna into cubes of about 2.5cms and mix with the marinade.

Leave to absorb the flavours for at least 30 minutes, but even better is to refrigerate overnight.

Preheat the BBQ.

Cut the vegetables into 2.5cm cubes or chunks and thread onto metal skewers, alternating with the pieces of tuna.

Brush with the marinade.

Grill for a minute or two on all sides until the fish is just cooked through.

Per serving: kcals 310
Carbs 20g Fat 13g Protein 29g

Serve with **Flageolet, Red Pepper and Guindilla Salad** (page 45), **Wholewheat Pita Bread** (page 128) and **Cucumber Raita** (page 126), or with **Quinoa, Bulgur and Broad Bean Pilaf** (page 71).

Beef, Pork and Lamb still feature in our weekly menus, including on fast days. I do tend to go for leaner cuts, but a little fat certainly adds flavour.

With its high protein content, meat is fabulous for being very satisfying and provides a centrepoint around which you can create fabulous sauces and use a great variety of vegetables.

Many in the western world eat far too much protein, which raises your IGF-1 levels - something that fasting helps to counteract. The advice given to Michael Mosley by Prof. Valter Longo is that we should be aiming for an intake of under 0.85 grams of protein for each kilo of body weight and ideally the majority should be plant-based sources. Note that figure is for the protein content only, not the weight of the piece of meat or whatever. I have including protein values throughout the recipes, so that you can calculate your intake if you wish.

For fast days I suggest using portion sizes of approximately 100g for a woman or 125g for a man.

Scandinavian Meatballs

Toulouse Sausage and Lentil Casserole

I love the meaty sausages that you can buy here in South West France, they come in one long continuous sausage, rather than as individual links and are made from just pork and seasoning, with no cereal fillers. Here, I have cooked them in a traditional style with lentils and vegetables.

Serves 6

600g Toulouse sausages 1860 kcals

1/2 tbsp sunflower oil 62 kcals

2 large onions, chopped 120 kcals

2 cloves garlic, chopped 9 kcals

3 sticks celery, chopped 19 kcals

2 large carrots, chopped 59 kcals

2 large tomatoes, skinned and chopped (see * Tip on facing page) 65 kcals

1 tbsp tomato puree 6 kcals

300g whole green lentils 315 kcals

150ml red wine 124 kcals

450ml water

Sea salt and freshly ground black pepper

Bouquet garni (bay leaf, parsley, thyme)

To garnish

1 tbsp parsley, finely chopped 1kcal

Soak lentils overnight in cold water (unless the packet says it is not necessary).

Preheat oven to 200c (fan).

Heat a large ovenproof casserole pan over medium heat and brown the sausage on both sides. Remove from the pan and cut into individual portions.

Add the oil to the pan and gently sauté the onion and garlic until soft and translucent. Add the celery and carrot and fry for 3 to 4 minutes more. Add the tomatoes and tomato purée and cook for 2 to 3 minutes longer.

Drain the lentils and add to the casserole, together with the bouquet garni and red wine.

Stir well and season with salt and pepper. Add water to cover, then put the sausages on top. Cover with a lid and bake for 30 to 40 minutes.

Serve sprinkled with chopped parsley.

Per serving: kcals 440
Carbs 21g Fat 24g Protein 29g

Serve with **Cauliflower Mash** (page 84) for another 52 kcals.

Beef and Carrot Casserole

The idea for this dish came from one of the ladies on the 5:2 Intermittent Fasting Diet group on Facebook, whose French grandmother "was simple in her approach, but delivered brilliant food". I have paired it with **Pommes Dauphinoise** (page 76) for a real taste of traditional style French fare.

Serves 6

1 tbsp olive oil 120 kcals

2 medium onions, roughly chopped 44 kcals

2 cloves garlic, finely chopped 8 kcals

800g stewing beef, cubed 1486 kcals

1 tbsp plain flour 38 kcals

Sea salt and freshly ground black pepper

300g organic carrots, sliced 123 kcals

100g button mushrooms, halved 21 kcals

2 peeled plum tomatoes, crushed 57 kcals

100ml water

250ml red wine 207 kcals

2 bay leaves

a few sprigs of thyme

2 tbsp chopped flat leaf parsley 3 kcals

Preheat the oven to 160c (fan).

Heat the oil in a cast iron casserole pot over medium heat and gently sauté the onions and garlic for a few minutes, until translucent and starting to colour.

Trim the beef to discard any gristle or excess fat.

Sprinkle flour over and season with salt and pepper.

Add to the pan in batches, stirring frequently, to seal the meat.

Then add the carrots, tomatoes, mushrooms, water and wine and mix together well.

Add the herbs and bring to the boil.

Cover with a lid, transfer to the oven and cook for at least 2 hours, checking occasionally in case it needs any more water.

Per serving: kcals 357
Carbs 13g Fat 11g Protein 43g

---

*Tip: to skin tomatoes, lightly slash the skin of each tomato with a sharp knife, then put into a bowl and cover with boiling water. Leave for at least 30 seconds, then remove with a slotted spoon and slip off the skin as soon as cool enough to handle.

Spice-rubbed Pork Escalope with Spring Onions

The idea for this recipe came from Allegra McEvedy in the Guardian. Fennel is an excellent partner for pork and combined with my favourite spices of cumin and coriander, I knew this was going to be a winner.

Serves 2

2 pork escalopes (90g each) 261 kcals

1 tsp fennel seeds 7 kcals

1/2 tsp cumin seeds 4 kcals

1/2 tsp coriander seeds

Sea salt and freshly ground black pepper

1 large spring onion, halved lengthwise 8 kcals

1/2 tbsp groundnut oil 60 kcals

Lightly crush the fennel, cumin and coriander seeds in a pestle and mortar, then mix in a little salt and plenty of black pepper.

Lay the escalopes on a chopping board and trim off any excess fat as necessary. Rub the spice mix all over the pork on both sides.

Heat a frying pan until hot, add the oil, then carefully add the escalopes. Cook for 3 to 5 minutes on each side, depending on thickness, then remove and rest on a warmed plate.

Add the spring onions to the pan and sauté gently until they have wilted and start to brown at the edges.

Serve the escalopes with the spring onions on top and any pan juices drizzled over.

Per serving: kcals 170
Carbs 2g Fat 6g Protein 28g

I served it on a bed of stir-fried peppers and onion with **Cucumber and Peanut Salsa** (page 125), Tomato Concasse and **Cheesy-topped Baked Sweet Potato** (page 78).

Herb-crusted Lamb Chops

The idea for this came from John Torode on Masterchef, where one of the challenges was to recreate his Venison Cutlets with Skordalia and a Beetroot and Jalapeno Relish. Here's my take on the idea, using lamb chops.

Serves 2

- 4 lamb chops 632 kcals
- 2 tbsp plain flour 57 kcals
- Sea salt and freshly ground black pepper
- 1 large egg 72 kcals
- 75g breadcrumbs 185 kcals
- 1 tbsp parsley, finely chopped 1 kcal
- 1 tbsp sage, finely chopped 6 kcals
- 1 tbsp sunflower oil 124 kcals

Trim the lamb chops to remove any unwanted fat.

Prepare 3 fairly flat dishes or bowls - one with seasoned flour, one with beaten egg and one with the breadcrumbs mixed with the herbs.

Dip each chop in flour, then coat with beaten egg and finally coat with breadcrumbs, patting them firmly to ensure that the breadcrumbs stick.

Heat the oil in a frying pan over medium heat and cook the chops for about 3 minutes on each side or until nicely browned and cooked to your taste.

Per serving (2 chops): kcals 539
Carbs 34g Fat 24g Protein 57g

(1 chop): kcals 382
Carbs 34g Fat 28g Protein 33g

Serve with **Garlic Mash** (page 82), **Piquant Beetroot Relish** (page 125) and steamed green beans.

Scandinavian Meatballs

Those of you who visit Ikea may have developed a liking for these.... A Danish friend shared her recipe with us, which uses a mix of beef and pork.

Makes about 40

For the meatballs

> **600g minced beef 1115 kcals**
>
> **400g minced pork 572 kcals**
>
> **2 onions, roughly chopped 88 kcals**
>
> **2 large eggs 143 kcals**
>
> **1 cup of flour or fresh breadcrumbs 427 kcals**
>
> **Sea salt and freshly ground black pepper**
>
> **1/2 tsp mixed spice (cinnamon, ginger, cloves and nutmeg)**

For frying

> **25g butter or vegetable oil 179 kcals**

Whizz the onions and eggs in a blender and then add the eggs, flour/breadcrumbs, seasoning and spices.

Put this mixture with the meat in a large bowl and work it with your hands, adding water as needed to get a firm mixture that holds together.

Let it rest for at least 15 minutes in the fridge.

Form into balls with your hands or using a spoon and then fry in butter until well browned all over.

To make different styles, add various spices, herbs or garlic - e.g. cumin, paprika and coriander for Moroccan kefta; garlic and mint for Greek keftedes; curry spices with garlic and ginger for Indian kofta; garlic, nutmeg for Spanish albondigas.

*Per meatball: kcals 64
Carbs 2g Fat 2g Protein 8g*

Albondigas Caseras ~ Spanish Meatballs

Here is one of the variations to the previous recipe in Spanish style, with a delicious sauce. Serve with rice or **Cauliflower Rice** page (84) or as Tapas.

Serves 4

For the meatballs

> **1/2 batch Scandinavian Meatballs (without mixed spice)**
>
> **4 cloves garlic, chopped 18 kcals**
>
> **1/2 tsp grated nutmeg 6 kcals**
>
> **Sea salt and freshly ground black pepper**

For frying

> **2 tbsp olive oil 240 kcals**

For the sauce

> **1 onion, coarsely chopped 44 kcals**
>
> **1 clove garlic, finely chopped 4 kcals**
>
> **1 green pepper, deseeded and cut in strips 24 kcals**
>
> **1 small tomato, skinned and chopped 16 kcals**
>
> **125ml dry white wine 103 kcals**
>
> **200ml chicken stock 8 kcals**
>
> **Sea salt and freshly ground black pepper**

Follow the method for **Scandinavian Meatballs** - adding the garlic along with the onions and using nutmeg instead of the mixed spice - up to the stage where they are well browned all over.

Add the onions, garlic and green pepper and cook until the onion has softened. Add the tomato, wine and stock and seasoning. Cover and simmer for 45 minutes.

*Per serving: kcals 413
Carbs 22g Fat 15g Protein 40g*

Lemony Lamb Kebabs

Making a marinade from onions, garlic, lemon and spices and whizzing it up in a food processor makes these kebabs wonderfully aromatic and flavourful. They cook quickly on the BBQ and make a complete meal with the pita bread.

Serves 2

> 200g boneless lamb, cut into 3cm cubes 372 kcals
>
> 2 Wholewheat Pita (page 128) 200 kcals

For the marinade:

> 1/2 onion, chopped 22 kcals
>
> 1 cloves garlic, crushed 4 kcals
>
> 15ml olive oil 120 kcals
>
> Juice of 1/2 lemon 12 kcals
>
> 1 tsp Cumin and Coriander Spice Mix (see box, this page) 8 kcals

For the Tsatsiki:

> 4 tbsp Greek yogurt 45 kcals
>
> 1/4 cucumber 11 kcals
>
> 1 tbsp mint leaves, finely chopped 3 kcals

For serving:

> 1 cup shredded lettuce 8 kcals
>
> 1/2 onion, sliced 22 kcals
>
> 1 tomato, sliced 11 kcals

Put all the marinade ingredients in a food processor and mix until well combined.

Mix lamb and marinade in a bowl, cover and refrigerate several hours or overnight.

Peel the cucumber, then cut into 4 lengthways and cut off and discard the seeds.

Chop finely and put into a sieve or colander over a bowl, sprinkle with salt and then cover with a small plate with a weight on top.

Leave to drain for about 15 minutes, then squeeze as much moisture as possible out.

Mix with the mint and put into a serving dish.

Preheat the BBQ or grill to hot.

Thread the lamb onto skewers.

Grill until nicely browned on the outside, but still slightly pink in the middle.

Serve in a **Wholewheat Pita** (page 128) with lettuce, sliced onion and sliced tomato with the **Tsatsiki** dressing and a wedge of lemon to squeeze over.

Per serving: kcals 420
Carbs 33g Fat 16g Protein 36g

As part of a Greek meal, the kebabs can be served with **Humus and Crudités** (page 29) and a **Greek Salad with Feta and Olives** (page 52).

Cumin and Coriander Spice Mix

This is a favourite combination of spices that I find works well with many different styles of cooking. It is if you like, my basic masala mix.

> 1 tbsp cumin seeds 23 kcals
>
> 1 tbsp coriander seeds 15 kcals

Heat a small frying pan over medium heat, then sprinkle in the seeds. Shake the pan frequently and cook until the seeds are starting to colour and release their aroma. Remove from the heat and grind coarsely in a pestle and mortar (or grinder). Store the mix in a screw top jar, or in a grinder ready to use for all kinds of savoury dishes.

Per tsp: kcals 6
Carbs 1g Fat 0g Protein 0g

Rump Steak with Garlic Mushrooms

We don't often eat red meat and I find even a small portion quite filling, so this seemed like it would be a good choice for a fast day, when it is helpful to eat protein, which the body cannot store.

Serves 2

> 200g rump steak 358 kcals
>
> 4 large mushrooms, chopped 20 kcals
>
> 1 clove garlic, finely chopped 4 kcals
>
> 1 tsp olive oil 40 kcals
>
> 2 tbsp water
>
> A bunch of watercress 4 kcals
>
> 1 blood orange 86 kcals
>
> 4 small tomatoes, halved 65 kcals
>
> 1 tsp balsamic vinegar 1 kcal

Cook the mushrooms in a frying pan with the faintest hint of olive oil and a couple of tablespoons of water.

Dry fry the steak for about 2 and a half minutes on each side.

Toss the watercress leaves with the juice from half the orange and release the segments from the other half with a sharp knife and add to the leaves along with a splash of balsamic vinegar.

Serve the steak with the mushrooms, the watercress leaves and add the tomatoes for a bit more colour.

Per serving: kcals 289
Carbs 20g Fat 9g Protein 35g

Serve with a spoonful of **Light Coleslaw** (page 43) for another 36 calories.

Pork and Noodle Stir Fry

This is a good way to use any leftover Roast Pork.

Serves 2

> 200g cooked pork, cubed 286 kcals
>
> 1 tbsp sunflower oil 124 kcals
>
> 1 onion, sliced 44 kcal
>
> 1/4 red bell pepper, cut into strips 9 kcals
>
> 1/4 cup of broccoli florets 7 kcal
>
> 2 mushrooms, sliced 8 kcals
>
> 30g mange tout, topped and tailed 10 kcals
>
> 1/4 tsp sesame oil 11 kcal
>
> 1 tbsp Tamari soy sauce 10 kcal
>
> 1 cup of baby spinach leaves 7 kcal
>
> 50g medium egg noodles 198 kcals

Cook the noodles in boiling water according to packet instructions, then drain, reserving some of the liquid.

Meanwhile, heat the sunflower oil in a wok or large frying pan on medium-high heat. Stir-fry the onion until translucent and softened, then add the pepper, broccoli, mushrooms and mange-tout. Stir-fry for a few minutes until all the vegetables are slightly tender but still have a bit of crunch.

Stir in the sesame oil and soy sauce, then add some of the liquid from the noodles to make a light sauce. Add the spinach and noodles and stir-fry for a minute or so until the spinach is wilted and the noodles heated through.

Serve immediately.

Per serving: kcals 354
Carbs 27g Fat 12g Protein 33g

Ham and Leek Stuffed Pancakes in Cheese Sauce

It is very useful to have some ready-made pancakes in the freezer, as they defrost quickly and can be stuffed with such a variety of savoury fillings. Topped with a mustardy cheese sauce and browned in the oven, they make a delicious meal. The filling can also be made ahead and frozen. This is a good way to use leftover cooked turkey or chicken as well, which could be mixed with ham or used instead.

Serves 4 (2 stuffed crepes each)

For the pancakes - makes 16 (freeze half for another time)

- **100g plain flour, sifted 364 kcals**
- **2 eggs 126 kcals**
- **300ml semi-skimmed milk 149 kcals**
- **A pinch of sea salt**
- **40g unsalted butter 287 kcals**

For the filling

- **10g unsalted butter 72 kcals**
- **300g leeks, washed and finely sliced 183 kcals**
- **150g mushrooms, cleaned and sliced 32 kcals**
- **300g cooked ham, chopped 489 kcals**
- **1/2 tsp Worcestershire sauce 3 kcals**
- **Freshly ground black pepper**

For the mustardy cheese sauce

- **15g unsalted butter 108 kcals**
- **15g plain flour 55 kcals**
- **300ml semi-skimmed milk 149 kcals**
- **1 tsp grainy mustard 3 kcals**
- **30g strong cheese, grated 121 kcals**
- **Freshly grated nutmeg**

- **1/2 tsp Tamari soy sauce 2 kcals**
- **Freshly ground black pepper**

For the asparagus fagots

- **12 asparagus spears, trimmed 116 kcals**
- **2 rashers of streaky bacon 160 kcals**

For the pancakes:

Put all flour, egg and milk into a blender and whizz until smooth. Leave to rest for 30 minutes.

Heat a little butter in a non-stick omelette pan, brush it round to coat thoroughly, get the pan really hot, then turn the heat down to medium and pour in enough mixture to coat the bottom (about 1 ladleful), tilting the pan to spread it evenly.

Cook for up to a minute until it starts to turn golden underneath, then flip over and cook the other side. Slide onto a plate and continue until all the mix is used up, layering a piece of greaseproof paper between the pancakes.

For the filling:

Melt the butter in a frying pan, add the leeks and cook gently, adding a splash of water if necessary, until the leeks are soft, stirring occasionally. Add the mushrooms and cook, stirring often, until they start to release their liquid. Add the ham and season with Worcestershire sauce and pepper. Set aside.

For the cheese sauce:
Melt the butter in a saucepan over low heat. Stir in the flour, and let it cook for two minutes, stirring.

Remove from the heat and start to add the milk, a very small amount to start with, beating in really thoroughly before adding a little more milk and beating that in.

Continue in this fashion until you have a smooth creamy consistency, by which time you can start to add the milk in larger amounts, each time stirring in thoroughly.

If it gets lumpy at any stage, then just continue beating until smooth before adding more milk.

When all the milk has been mixed in, bring to the boil, reduce the heat and simmer for a few minutes, until you have a good consistency.

Stir in the mustard, soy sauce, nutmeg and cheese, then season with salt and pepper as needed.

For the asparagus fagots:

Blanch the asparagus in boiling water for 2 minutes, then refresh under cold water.

Pat dry then make two bundles, wrapping each with the bacon, then put on a baking sheet.
To complete the dish:

Preheat the oven to 180c (fan).

Divide the filling between the pancakes, rolling them up and putting them into a greased ovenproof dish.

Pour the sauce over the top.

Bake for about 30 minutes until melted and bubbling and the crepes are heated through.

Put the asparagus fagots in the oven for the last 10 minutes of the cooking time.

Per serving: kcals 488
Carbs 39g Fat 25g Protein 29g

Freeze the remaining pancakes, wrapping well in cling film and storing a plastic bag.

Serve with **Fennel and Radish Salad** (page 51).

Lean Lamb Stir-Fry with Feta

I had 3 lean leg steaks in the freezer. After trimming them to remove all separable fat, I had enough meat for our main fast day dish, plus a slightly larger amount for **Lemony Lamb Kebabs** (page 106) the following day. Saves £££s as well as pounds, this way of eating!

Serves 2

> **165g lean boneless leg of lamb, cubed 338 kcals**
> **1 tsp cumin and coriander spice mix (page 106)**
> **1 medium onion, sliced 42 kcals**
> **1 clove garlic, finely chopped 4 kcals**
> **3 small carrots, sliced 21 kcals**
> **3 sticks celery, sliced 14 kcals**
> **120g cauliflower florets 30 kcals**
> **2 large tomatoes, cut into 1/8ths 32 kcals**
> **2 large mushrooms, sliced 18 kcals**
> **135g spinach, roughly shredded 31 kcals**
> **80g savoy cabbage (about a 1/4 of a whole head), cut into strips 19 kcals**
> **1/2 tbsp extra virgin olive oil 60 kcals**
> **Seasoning to taste**
> **25g feta cheese, cubed 66 kcal**

Rub the spices over the lamb and set aside while you prepare the vegetables.

Heat half the olive oil in a wok over medium heat and fry the lamb until nicely browned on all sides, then remove and set aside.

Add the onions and garlic and stir-fry for a couple of minutes.

Next add the carrots, celery and cauliflower and cook a few more minutes.

Add the mushrooms and tomatoes and continue to stir-fry as the tomatoes break down and start to release their liquid.

You may need to add a little water if they are not particularly juicy, but try not to dilute the luscious flavours too much!

Next add the cabbage and give that a minute or so before you add the spinach.

Before the spinach has completely wilted down, return the lamb to the pan and mix together well.

Divide into two portions and add sliced or crumbled feta to the top (this makes such a difference to the overall enjoyment of the dish, don't be tempted to omit it - if you have some spare calories, you might like a bit more!).

Per serving: kcals 379
Carbs 31g Fat 19g Protein 25g

We eat chicken fairly often and where possible I choose organic or free-range - not only for a good flavour, but for the better care the birds are given, the more natural type of food that they have eaten and the lack of growth-promoters used.

Turkey escalopes are very lean and low fat so make a good centrepiece for a fast day meal and can take the place of pork or veal. I sometimes use minced turkey as an alternative to minced beef.

In this region of South West France there is an abundance of ducks, so duck meat also features on the menu, especially when we have guests for dinner.

Asian Poached Chicken with Light Caesar Salad

Chicken Satay

This satay sauce recipe developed from available ingredients, but I do remember that the first version that I made was from a series of Robert Carrier magazines that my mother collected.

Serves 4

500g chicken breast fillet 570 kcals

Juice of 1/2 lemon 12 kcals

1/2 tsp turmeric 4 kcals

1/2 tsp curry powder 3 kcals

2 tsp Tamari soy sauce 7 kcals

1 tsp sesame oil 40 kcals

1 tbsp rice wine (or dry sherry or dry white wine) 25 kcals

For the Cucumber Pickle:

½ cucumber, peeled and sliced 23 kcals

1 tbsp rice wine (or cider) vinegar 2 kcals

1 tsp caster sugar 16 kcals

To serve:

1/2 batch of Satay Sauce (page 126) 40 kcals

A bunch of spring onions, finely sliced lengthwise 19 kcals

Put the cucumber slices in a shallow dish.

Mix the sugar with the vinegar and pour over the cucumber. Leave to absorb the flavours for an hour or so. Sprinkle with salt just before serving.

To prepare the chicken breast, first trim off any fat, then slice the meat on the diagonal and at an angle, so that you have very thin slices (about 5mm thick), this allows the chicken to cook quickly.

Mix together the marinade ingredients and coat the chicken thoroughly. Chill overnight or for several hours - at a push at least half an hour.

Thread the meat onto the skewers, using no more than 4 pieces per skewer, so they are not too crowded.

Preheat the BBQ or grill and grill the meat, turning several times, until thoroughly cooked through and lightly coloured.

Per serving: kcals 220
Carbs 8g Fat 8g Protein 29g

Serve with **Bean Shoot Salad** (page 52).

Cucumber Pickle

Satay Sauce (page 126)

Skewered Duck with Chilli, Garlic and Hoisin Sauce

Here in South West France they raise a lot of ducks. One of the ways in which the meat is sold is as "aiguillettes", which are fine fillets of meat, cut from the breast. It makes it very easy to prepare them in a marinade ready to be briefly barbecued. If you can't find these strips ready prepared, you can cut them from a breast or "magret". With duck being popular in both Asia and France, it makes a good candidate for fusion recipes.

Serves 2

190g duck fillets 353 kcals

For the marinade

1 clove garlic, finely chopped 4 kcals

2.5cm piece of root ginger, peeled and grated 8 kcals

1 hot red chilli, deseeded and finely chopped 3 kcals

1 tbsp hoisin sauce 35 kcals

1 tsp sesame oil 40 kcals

1 tbsp dry white wine 12 kcals

1 tbsp Tamari soy sauce 11 kcals

1/2 tsp cumin and coriander spice mix (page 106) 3 kcals

Mix the marinade ingredients in a bowl and add the duck fillets, ensuring they are well coated.

Cover the dish with clingfilm and leave to marinade for at least 30 minutes, but preferably for several hours in the fridge.

Preheat a barbecue or grill to very hot.

Thread each fillet onto a metal skewer and brush well with the marinade.

Grill for 1 or 2 minutes on each side only, as the duck should still be slightly pink in the middle.

Keep warm and leave to rest while you make the sauce.

Put any remaining marinade in a hot frying pan and sizzle to cook the chilli, garlic and ginger, adding some water to make a good consistency of sauce.

Per serving: kcals 236
Carbs 6g Fat 17g Protein 15g

Serve with a pile of steamed vegetables and a rocket salad with fresh cherries.

Chicken and Lemon Tagine

The preserved lemons and olives give this dish a real tang. You need something to contrast with the sauce, like cous-cous, rice, or flat bread like **Maneesh** (page 130). I've shown it here with green olives, but actually I think I prefer it with black ones. You can use chicken breast, but it is more traditional to use meat on the bone.

Serves 4

> 1 tbsp oil 120 kcals
>
> 1 large onion, diced 60 kcals
>
> 1 tsp ground cumin 8 kcals
>
> 1 tsp coriander
>
> 1 tsp paprika 6 kcals
>
> 1 tsp cinnamon 6 kcals
>
> 1 tsp turmeric 8 kcals
>
> 3 cloves garlic, crushed 13 kcals
>
> 4 skinless on the bone chicken joints 840 kcals
>
> 300ml good chicken stock 25 kcals
>
> 5 tbsp chopped coriander leaf 1 kcal
>
> 3 tbsp flat leaf parsley 4 kcals
>
> Sea salt and freshly ground black pepper
>
> 10 olives 51 kcals
>
> 2 preserved lemons, cut into thin strips 34 kcals
>
> 1 red chilli, seeded and finely sliced 8 kcals

To garnish

> 1 tbsp chopped coriander leaf

You can use a tagine dish for this or a heavy pan with a lid.

Start by frying the onions really slowly in the oil until they are soft but not coloured, then add the spices and garlic and fry for a couple of minutes stirring the whole time.

If you have time rub this mixture into the chicken and pop it into the fridge to marinade for a few hours.

Add the chicken to the pan and fry until the chicken just turns white, this should take just a couple of minutes.

Now add the stock, the coriander and parsley and season well.

Cover and simmer for 10 minutes on a really low heat.

Whilst all that's going on put the olives into a small bowl and cover them with boiling water, this will remove the salty residue from the olives.

Leave for a few minutes and then drain.

Now throw the preserved lemon strips and olives (and chilli if using) into the pan with the chicken and simmer until the chicken is lovely and soft.

Finish with a sprinkle of coriander.

Per serving: kcals 296
Carbs 10g Fat 20g Protein 20g

Black Pepper Chicken Sticks with Spicy Tomato Dipping Sauce

This makes a tasty sharing platter for summer picnic or barbecue or can be served as an appetiser. The idea came from a BBC Good Food recipe, but this version is a lot lower in calories.

Makes about 20

> 3 boneless, skinless chicken breasts 410 kcals
>
> Freshly ground black pepper
>
> Sea salt
>
> 1 tsp sesame oil 40 kcals

For the dipping sauce

500g ripe tomatoes, roughly chopped 89 kcals

1 green chilli, de-seeded and chopped

4 cloves garlic, peeled and chopped 18 kcals

50g raisins 150 kcals

A knob of ginger, peeled and chopped 4 kcals

30g raw cane brown sugar 113 kcals

1 tbsp walnut vinegar 3 kcals

1 tbsp fish sauce 6 kcals

a dash or two of Tabasco, to taste

Put some wooden skewers to soak in cold water, for at least 30 minutes.

Put the tomatoes, chilli, garlic, raisins and ginger into a food processor and blend to a rough purée.

Transfer to a saucepan and cook gently for about 30 minutes, until thickened.

Check the seasoning and add a little Tabasco if you want it a bit hotter.

Leave to cool.

Heat a barbecue or grill.

Slice the chicken breasts into strips about 5mm thick, cutting diagonally across to get them fairly wide.

Put one piece onto each skewer and brush with sesame oil.

Season generously with black pepper and a little sea salt.

Grill the skewers on both sides until cooked through; it should only take a couple of minutes each side.

The chicken skewers can be served hot or cold with the cool dipping sauce.

Per serving: kcals 42
Carbs 5g Fat 1g Protein 4g

Baked Jerk-Spiced Chicken

I have a favourite jerk spice mix, which I was given by friends visiting from St John, in the US Virgin Islands, which is flavourful without being too hot. The technique of 'washing' the chicken with lemon or lime juice is one that I picked up in the Caribbean. It helps the spice to stick to the chicken.

Serves 2

2 chicken breast fillets (100g each), no skin 202 kcals

1/2 lemon or lime, juice only 6 kcals

2 tsp jerk seasoning

Preheat the oven to 200c (fan).

Trim the chicken of any fat.

Put the lemon or lime juice into a bowl and roll the chicken in it, ensuring that it is completely covered.

Transfer the chicken to a non-stick baking sheet and sprinkle the spice mix generously over both sides.

Bake for 20 minutes or until cooked all the way through.

Per serving: kcals 104
Carbs 1g Fat 2g Protein 19g

Serve sliced on top of **Quinoa, Bulgur and Broad Bean Pilaf** (page 71) and with a mixed salad, or as shown here, with **Summer Squash Slices** (page 83).

Turkey, Red Bean and Chocolate Chilli

I love Mexican flavours – what an excellent excuse to add a good grating of dark chocolate to your food! I used lean turkey, but you could use beef, soya mince or quorn. It was my sister who showed me the way to add the flour to the cumin seeds for thickening the sauce. I must have been making variations of this for over 40 years now! It is a spicy and delicious family favourite.

I was lucky to be given a block of 100% cacao Venezuelan Black chocolate by some appreciative guests – a great ingredient that lasts for ages, as a little goes a long way. A dusting on a dessert is lovely but it is also very good in savoury dishes such as this. Just adds that little something, but hardly any calories.

Serves 4

    1 tbsp olive oil 120 kcals

    1 onion, chopped 46 kcals

    1 clove garlic, finely chopped 4 kcals

    350g lean turkey (or soya mince or quorn) 372 kcals

    1/2 tsp Mexican chilli powder 4 kcals

    1/2 tsp smoked paprika 3 kcals

    200g peeled plum tomatoes, roughly chopped 43 kcals

    400g can red kidney beans, drained 211 kcals

    Sea salt and freshly ground black pepper

    1/2 tsp cumin seeds 4 kcals

    1/2 tbsp plain flour 14 kcals

    10g grated dark chocolate (100% cacao) 20 kcals

    1 tbsp chopped coriander leaves 5 kcals

If using turkey, chop finely or mince in a food processor.

Heat the olive oil in a heavy-bottomed pan and gently sauté the onions and garlic until soft and golden.

Add the turkey or vegetarian alternative and stir-fry until lightly coloured all over.

Add the chill and paprika and mix well. Pour in the tomatoes and beans and bring to a simmer.

Check the seasoning, then cook for 15 - 20 minutes, adding a little water if necessary.

Grind the cumin seeds in a pestle and mortar and stir in the flour. Spoon in sufficient liquid from the chilli to make a smooth paste.

Stir in to the chilli and cook for 2 or 3 minutes more, stirring often, to thicken the sauce.

Transfer to a serving dish, grate the chocolate over and garnish with chopped coriander.

Per serving: kcals 211
Carbs 17g Fat 5g Protein 25g

A Mexican style meal
(from right to left)
shredded lettuce,
sliced spring onion,
low fat fromage frais,
Guacamole (page 28),
grated cheese,
tomato salsa
and a few taco chips.

Baked Citrus Chicken with Pumpkin, Parsnips and Peppers

The idea here is to have the enjoyment of a roast chicken, but by using citrus juice instead of fat, the whole meal is lighter and healthier. When there are just the 2 of us for lunch, I can get several meals from an average sized bird, and then there is the carcass to make stock with for a tasty soup. A great alternative to a traditional Sunday Roast!

Serves 4

> 1 whole chicken (1.5kg) 917 kcals
>
> 2 oranges 40 kcals
>
> 1 lime 20 kcals
>
> 500g pumpkin or butternut squash 170 kcals
>
> 1 med-large (200g) parsnip 150 kcals
>
> 1 red bell pepper 37 kcals
>
> 1 red onion 44 kcals
>
> 1 red chilli 6 kcals
>
> 1 tbsp jerk seasoning
>
> 1 tsp Bisto gravy powder (optional) 5 kcals
>
> 300 ml vegetable stock or water

Heat the oven to 180C (fan).

Remove any visible fat from the chicken.

Peel the pumpkin or squash, the parsnip and the red onion. Trim the pepper and chilli and remove the seeds and pith. Cut all the veggies into wedges and put into a roasting tray.

Make slivers from some of the orange and lime peel (no pith) and reserve.

Lightly grate the remainder over the veggies.

Squeeze the juice of the fruits and pour half over the veggies.

Put the chicken on top and brush the remainder of the juice over, then rub in the jerk seasoning.

Bake for 1 to 1.5 hours, until the chicken is cooked through, basting regularly with the juice.

Put the chicken to rest on a warm serving plate and keep the veggies warm while you make the gravy.

If there is any visible fat in the pan juices, strain it off.

Add stock or water to the pan together with the orange and lime rind.

I like to use a little Bisto mixed with water to make the gravy a little thicker, but it will have a good colour anyway from the jerk spices.

Bring to the boil and simmer for few minutes whilst steaming other veggies to serve with it.

Serve slices or portions of meat without skin, the wonderful coloured vegetables alongside and gravy with some of the peel to bring the whole dish together.

You could use sweet potato or beetroot instead of parsnip.

Based on a recipe in an old Good Housekeeping cookery club book *"Healthy Eating"*, 1995.

Per serving: 349 kcals
Carb 30g Fat 9g Protein 38g

Serve with steamed vegetables such as julienne carrots, broccoli spears and peas.

Asian Poached Chicken

I discovered the joys of poached chicken when one of our Images of France photography course guests introduced me to the work of a New Zealand cook, Annabel Langbein. Her book, *"Cooking to Impress without Stress"* not only has a fabulous title, it also contains some excellent ideas, of which this is one.

I love the fact that this is an easy and low fat way to prepare chicken. The flesh is moist and full of flavour. Then there is the added bonus of having tasty stock made at the same time, which makes home made soups even better. You could use the same method to cook just a single chicken breast, or a joint or two.

The slightly spicy aromatic flavour of this goes particularly well with **Raw Vegetable Salad with Vietnamese Dressing** (page 46), or I serve it with **Light Caesar Salad** (page 51).

> 1 whole organic or free range chicken
>
> 2 dried chillies
>
> 3 star anise
>
> 2.5cm of root ginger, cut into fine slices (no need to peel)
>
> 2 or 3 spring onions, or leek trimmings
>
> Sea salt and black pepper
>
> 12 whole mixed peppercorns
>
> Cold water, to cover.

Put the whole chicken into a large pan with the spices and flavourings, cover completely with cold water and bring to the boil.

Simmer very gently for 25 minutes, removing any scum that forms on the top.

Then remove from the heat, cover with a lid and leave to cool in the liquid.

Lift out the chicken when completely cool and store in the fridge until ready to use.

Remove the flavourings from the stock with a slotted spoon and discard.

Bring the stock to the boil and reduce to about half the volume, then strain and refrigerate.

Per 100g serving: kcals 200
Carbs 0g Fat 8g Protein 33g

As an alternative to the Asian flavourings, you could poach the chicken with bay leaves, thyme, parsley, and onion.

Enchiladas with Turkey

Delicious Mexican flavours with a zingy tomato sauce. You can use chicken instead of turkey, or a vegetarian mince instead.

Makes 6

> 1 batch of Turkey and Red Bean Chilli (page 116) 1266 kcals
>
> 6 tortillas 600 kcals
>
> 50g grated cheese (Red Leicester) 202 kcals

For the tomato sauce

> 400g plum tomatoes, peeled and chopped 92 kcals
>
> 1 red chilli, blackened and chopped 3 kcals
>
> 50g canned green chillies, chopped 17 kcals
>
> 1 onion, quartered 44 kcals
>
> 1 clove garlic, roughly chopped 4 kcals
>
> 2 tsp olive oil 80 kcals
>
> A pinch of cinnamon
>
> Sea salt

Make the chilli according to the **Turkey and Red Bean Chilli** recipe (page 116).

To make the tomato sauce:

Put the tomatoes, red and green chillies, onion, garlic and fresh tomato in a food processor and blend until finely chopped.

Heat the oil in a heavy pan, add the purée and stir-fry for a couple of minutes.

Add the cinnamon and salt, lower the heat and cook slowly for 15 minutes, stirring occasionally.

To make the enchiladas:

Preheat the oven to 180c (fan).

One at a time, soften the tortilla in a dry frying pan over medium heat, lift out with tongs and dip both sides into the tomato sauce, then transfer to an ovenproof dish.

Fill with some of the chilli mixture, fold in the sides and roll up, pushing to the end of the dish.

Repeat until all the enchiladas and chilli are used up.

Pour the sauce over the top and sprinkle with grated cheese.

Bake in the oven for about 30 minutes until well heated and the cheese is melted.

1 enchilada: kcals 384 Carbs 41g Fat 15g Protein 22g

Serve with a crisp green salad and garnish with a dollop of crème fraîche, a spoonful of **Guacamole** (page 28), some finely sliced radishes and sliced raw onions.

Curry accompaniments - Fresh Tomato, Red Onion and Coriander Chutney and Mint Raita

Chicken and Vegetable Curry

This is a quick and easy to make curry, using a ready-made curry paste and frozen vegetables. Make it special by putting some effort into the accompaniments.

Serves 4

> **1 tbsp sunflower oil 124 kcals**
>
> **550g chicken breast, cubed 348 kcals**
>
> **100g Tikka Masala Curry Paste 277 kcals**
>
> **384g mixed vegetables, chopped (fresh or frozen) 182 kcals**
>
> **150g tinned chopped tomatoes 33 kcals**

Heat the oil in a heavy pan, add the curry paste, mix in the chicken and sauté until sealed on all sides.

Add a splash of water if necessary to stop it burning.

Add the vegetables and tomatoes and mix well, bring to the boil, then lower the heat and simmer for 20 to 30 minutes, until the chicken is tender and the sauce reduced.

Per serving: kcals 241 Carbs 12g Fat 11g Protein 23g

To vary this recipe, add some light coconut milk, or some cooked yellow lentils or chickpeas.

Serve with **Fresh Tomato, Red Onion and Coriander Chutney** (page 126), **Mint Raita** (page 126) and **Naan Bread** (page 128).

119

Mushroom Stuffed Chicken Breast

Mushrooms, garlic and Serrano ham transform a simple chicken breast into a tasty dinner for a 5:2 fast day. Wrapping the chicken in ham and then in foil helps to keep it nice and moist during cooking.

Serves 1

100g chicken breast 164 kcals

2 medium mushrooms, finely chopped 8 kcals

1 clove garlic, finely chopped 4 kcals

1 tsp olive oil 40 kcals

A pinch of ground cumin 1 kcal

1 tsp chopped coriander leaves 5 kcals

Sea salt and freshly ground black pepper

1 tsp pesto 23 kcals

1 slice Serrano ham, trimmed of fat 36 kcals

To serve

4 asparagus spears 19 kcals

1/2 medium carrot 13 kcals

A handful of broad beans, podded 18 kcals

100g cauliflower florets 26 kcals

5g crème fraîche 11 kcals

Heat the oven to 180c (fan).

Heat the oil in a frying pan and gently sauté the garlic for a minute or so and then add the mushrooms.

Stir fry until the mushrooms are just cooked and starting to release their moisture.

Remove from the heat and season with cumin, coriander leaf and season to taste.

Trim the chicken breast to the required size and remove any fat.

Cut a diagonal slice into the thickest part of the flesh, without cutting all the way through, to make a pocket.

Stuff the mushroom filling into the pocket and spread the pesto over the chicken.

Prepare a sheet of baking paper or foil, (about 30cm square) and lay the Serrano ham in the middle.

Put the chicken on top and then wrap the ham around it to help hold it together.

Wrap up and seal the foil or baking paper, crimping the edges together, place on a baking tray and cook for 30 minutes.

Meanwhile, boil the broad beans for 3 to 4 minutes until tender, then refresh under cold water and slip off their skins, unless they are tiny.

Boil the cauliflower until tender, steaming the asparagus and carrots over the top, then mash the cauliflower with the crème fraîche.

Unwrap the chicken and serve with a little sauce made by adding some of the cauliflower water to the residue left in the foil.

Per serving: kcals 403
Carbs 15g Fat 18g Protein 45g

Adjust your chicken portion according to your available calories or appetite!

You can use Parma Ham (prosciutto) or Bayonne Ham instead of Serrano.

Chicken with Saffron and Garlic ~ Pollo al Ajillo

This is another recipe from Penelope Casas excellent *"Tapas"* book. The flavours of saffron and garlic are wonderfully aromatic and bring a taste of sunshine to a dull day. I served this as a main meal, but you could equally present it as an appetiser for 6 - 8 people. I've shown it here cooked on the bone, but the calorie count would be lower if using breast meat, in which case, cut it into large chunks.

Serves 4

500g chicken (2 legs and 2 wings) 1110 kcals

1 tbsp olive oil 120 kcals

4 cloves garlic, peeled 18 kcals

1 tbsp brandy 33 kcals

1/2 tsp plain flour 5 kcals

2 tbsp dry white wine 24 kcals

2 tbsp stock or water 1 kcal

Sea salt

1 tbsp finely chopped flat-leaf parsley 1 kcal

A pinch of saffron strands

3 black peppercorns 1 kcal

Discard the wing tips and divide the wings into two and cut the legs into thighs and drumsticks, or if using breast meat, cut into large chunks.

Heat the oil in a frying pan over medium heat.

Add the garlic and chicken pieces and sauté, removing the garlic when it is golden and setting it aside in a mortar and continuing to cook the chicken until it is browned on all sides.

Add the brandy to the pan, stand well back and ignite.

Then sprinkle in the flour and add the wine, water and salt.

Cover and simmer for 15 minutes.

Make a paste of the garlic with the saffron, pepper, parsley and a little salt.

Add this mixture in with the chicken and cook for a further 15 minutes.

Per serving: kcals 328
Carbs 2g Fat 14g Protein 42g

Serve with **Patatas Bravas** (page 78) and **Cabbage, Green Pepper and Caraway Salad** (page 50).

Chicken, Chorizo and Butter Bean

The addition of the beans and chorizo makes this a substantial dish with robust Spanish flavourings.

Serves 2

300g chicken breast fillet 330 kcals

1/2 tsp smoked paprika 4 kcals

30g chorizo 105 kcals

2 cloves garlic, finely chopped 9 kcals

150g courgettes, sliced 30 kcals

200g tomatoes, peeled and chopped 76 kcals

120g cooked butter beans 97 kcals

2 tsp olive oil 84 kcals

To garnish

Some chopped coriander or flat parsley leaves

Trim the chicken breast and sprinkle all over with the smoked paprika.

Peel the skin off the chorizo and cut into slices.

Heat the oil in a heavy pan and add the chicken and chorizo, turning and frying until the chicken is sealed on all sides and the chorizo is starting to release oil.

Add the garlic and courgettes and cook for a few more minutes.

Add the tomatoes, parsley and butter beans and add a couple of tablespoonfuls of water.

Bring to the boil, then cover and simmer over low heat for about 30 minutes, until the chicken is tender.

Garnish with chopped coriander or parsley.

This looks good served in a cazuela, a flat earthenware dish used extensively in Spain.

Per serving kcals 368
Carbs 19g Fat 11g Protein 45g

Serve with **Cauliflower and Caper Salad** (page 42) and **Cabbage, Green Pepper and Raisin Salad** (page 50).

Watercress and Fresh Cabécou Goats' Cheese

123

Sauces and Dressings

Balsamic and Walnut Vinaigrette

This is a slightly modified version of my popular Berty Salad Dressing. I have lowered the ratio of oil to vinegar to keep the calorie count low for fast days.

Makes 165 ml

- 1 tsp Maldon sea salt flakes
- 1 clove garlic, peeled 4 kcals
- 1 tsp grainy mustard 4 kcals
- 1 tsp freshly ground black pepper 6 kcals
- 4 tbsp aged balsamic vinegar 12 kcal
- 4 tbsp white wine vinegar or walnut vinegar 12 kcal
- 2 tbsp extra virgin olive oil 240 kcals

Using a pestle and mortar, crush the garlic into the salt to make a smooth puree.

Add the other ingredients and mix well.

Transfer to a screw top bottle or jar and shake well.

Shake well just before using.

I find it keeps well in the larder.

Per serving (1 tbsp): kcals 26
Carbs 0g Fat 3g Protein 0g

Pepper, Chilli and Mango Salsa

This salsa goes well with vegetarian, fish or meat dishes. I sometimes substitute peach for mango, as it is a lot easier to find here in the summer. You could also make it with canned peaches and pre-prepared strips of red pepper, which you can find in jars. Any leftovers work well to mix in with some cooked rice to make a tasty rice salad.

Serves 4

- ½ a mango, finely chopped 136 kcals
- 1 red pepper, grilled and skinned, finely chopped 36 kcals
- 1 small hot red chilli, deseeded and finely chopped 4 kcals
- ½ red onion, finely chopped 24 kcals
- 1 clove garlic, crushed 4 kcals
- Chopped fresh basil and coriander leaves
- Juice of ½ a lime 20 kcals
- 1 tsp olive oil 40 kcals
- Sea salt and freshly ground black pepper

I use a blowtorch to blacken the skin of the pepper all over, then pop it into plastic bag and wrap it up in a cloth to keep warm.

After about 10 minutes, the skin is easy to scrape away.

Mix all the ingredients together and season to taste with salt and pepper.

Serve with Oaty Chickpea Crumble

Per serving: kcals 66
Carbs 14g Fat 2g Protein 1g

Light Teriyaki Sauce

Serves 4

- 1 tbsp Tamari soy sauce 15 kcals
- 25g Hoisin sauce 58 kcals
- OR if not available, use
- - 1 tbsp Tamari soy sauce
- - 1 tsp honey or maple syrup
- - a pinch of Chinese five spice powder
- 2.5cm root ginger, peeled and finely chopped or grated 2 kcals
- 4 tbsp water
- 1 clove garlic, crushed 4 kcals

Mix all ingredients together and simmer in a small pan until the garlic and ginger have softened.

Leftovers can be stored for a few days in a covered container in the fridge. You can use this as a marinade for chicken, fish or tofu, or as a sauce in a vegetable stir-fry. It is used in my recipe for **Salmon Teriyaki with Leeks** (page 96).

Per serving: kcals 20
Carbs 4g Fat 0g Protein 1g

Cucumber and Peanut Salsa

There is an affinity between fresh cucumber and toasted peanuts and this happy combination works well as an accompaniment to **Spice-Rubbed Pork with Spring Onions**, see page 103.

Serves 2

 20g unsalted peanuts 113 kcals

 1/2 a cucumber 23 kcals

 sea salt

 1 tbsp coriander leaves, finely chopped

 1 red chilli, finely chopped 6 kcals

 1 spring onion, finely chopped 5 kcals

 juice of 1 lime 11 kcals

Grate the cucumber into a sieve or colander, sprinkle with salt and set over a bowl.

Put a plate on top with a weight (a can or jar of something will do) and leave for about 15 minutes.

Meanwhile, dry roast the peanuts on baking tray in a hot oven or in a dry frying pan, shaking occasionally, until evenly golden brown.

Squeeze the cucumber and discard the juice.

Mix the cucumber with the chilli, spring onion, chopped coriander and the lime juice.

Crush the peanuts lightly.

Serve the cucumber with the peanuts sprinkled on top.

Per serving: kcals 79
Carbs 7g Fat 5g Protein 4g

Piquant Beetroot Relish

This spicy beetroot relish goes really well with the **Herb-Crusted Lamb Chops** (page 104) or **Peppered Mackerel with Horseradish** (page 88).

Serves 4

 1 tsp olive oil 40 kcals

 1/2 red onion, chopped 22 kcals

 2 pickled jalapeno peppers, chopped 3 kcals

 300g cooked and peeled beetroot, chopped 132 kcals

 handful of coriander (cilantro), chopped 5 kcals

 handful of mint leaves, chopped 2 kcals

 25g walnut pieces, chopped 155 kcals

 2 tsp walnut or sherry vinegar 12 kcals

 2 tbsp water

Heat the oil in a frying pan and gently sauté the onion and chilli for a few minutes until softened.

Add the beetroot, herbs and walnuts and cook over low heat for about 15 minutes.

Add the vinegar and cook for a couple more minutes, then add the water.

Blend to a smooth paste in a food processor.

Turn into a serving dish and garnish with a sprig of mint or coriander.

Per serving: kcals 93
Carbs 11g Fat 5g Protein 3g

Fresh Tomato, Red Onion and Coriander Chutney

This is a refreshing side dish to go with a curry and one I would make to go with a take-away or alongside a home-made dish like my **Chicken and Vegetable Curry** (page 119)

Serves 4

> 1 medium tomato, finely chopped 22 kcals
>
> 1 small red onion, finely chopped 28 kcals
>
> 2 tbsp coriander leaf, finely chopped 5 kcals
>
> sea salt and freshly ground black pepper

Mix ingredients together, season to taste and leave for flavours to infuse for 30 minutes or so.

Per serving: kcals 14
Carbs 3g Fat 0g Protein 1g

Mint Raita

Serve with any curry dish along with flame-grilled or microwaved Poppadums, Mango Chutney and Lime Pickle. Greek yogurt gives a lovely smooth texture, but you can use low-fat yogurt too. I do use fresh mint if I can get it, but it is quick and easy to prepare with ready-made mint sauce.

Serves 4

> 125g natural yogurt 89 kcals
>
> 1 tsp ready-prepared mint sauce 6kcals
>
> -or
>
> 1 handful of mint leaves
>
> a pinch of sugar and sea salt

If using mint leaves, put them together with the sugar and salt in a mini processor or crush to a paste with a pestle and mortar.

Beat the yogurt so that it is smooth and add the mint sauce.

Garnish with ground spices, such as cumin and paprika and a tiny sprig of mint.

Per serving: kcals 24
Carbs 2g Fat 1g Protein 2g

A variation of this is Cucumber Raita.

Cucumber Raita

This makes a delightfully cooling and refreshing accompaniment to a hot, spicy curry.

> 1/2 large cucumber, peeled, deseeded and finely chopped 17 kcals
>
> 1 batch of Mint Raita (page 126)

Put peeled, deseeded and finely chopped cucumber into a sieve, sprinkle with salt and set over a bowl.

Cover with a plate and put a weight on top (a can of food perhaps).

Leave to drain for 30 minutes, then stir in to the Mint Raita.

Per serving: kcals 28
Carbs 4g fat 1g Protein 2g

Satay Sauce

Indispensable sauce for **Chicken Satay Skewers** (page 112) or to go with **Raw Vegetable Salad** (page 46).

Serves 8

> 200 ml light coconut cream 260 kcals
>
> 50g crunchy peanut butter 333 kcals
>
> 1/2 tsp curry powder 3 kcals
>
> 1/2 tsp chilli powder 6 kcals
>
> 1/4 tsp turmeric 2 kcals
>
> juice of half a lime 5 kcals
>
> 1 tbsp Tamari soy sauce 15 kcals
>
> 1 tsp maple syrup 16 kcals

Put the coconut cream into a saucepan over low heat with the spices and peanut butter.

Heat gently, stirring, until smooth.

Add the lime juice, soy sauce and maple syrup and adjust seasonings to taste.

Put into a bowl to cool until required.

Store in a screw top jar in the fridge.

Per serving: kcals 80
Carbs 2g Fat 7g Protein 2g

Bread

I make no apologies for the fact that I use a breadmaker. It is a wonderful time saver and makes fabulous dough! I think that if you make the dough by hand though, you will generally need to use more yeast than I have specified in the recipes.

I use local organically-grown stoneground strong wholewheat flour (Type 110) for most of my breads.

Wholewheat Pita Bread

Wholewheat pita bread is impossible to buy locally in SW France and the long life packs of white pita are rather too stodgy for my liking. Looking in the recipe book for my Panasonic Bread Maker, I was delighted to find that their recipe was for wholewheat flour and has no added fat.

Makes 8 small pita

   250g strong wholewheat flour, preferably organic stone-ground 793 kcals

   1/2 tsp yeast

   1/2 tsp sugar 8 kcals

   1/2 tsp salt

   150ml water

Let the bread-maker to do its Pizza Dough programme.

Preheat the oven to 220c (fan).

Divide the mix into 8.

Roll out using a little extra flour and leave to prove on a baking sheet for about 10 minutes, then bake in a hot oven for about 8 minutes, until puffed up and starting to colour.

Per serving: kcals 100
Carbs 19g Fat 0g Protein 0g

Wholewheat Sunflower Bread

Makes 1 loaf / 12 slices

For the dough:

   3/4 tsp fast acting yeast 9 kcals

   400g stoneground organic wholewheat flour 1356 kcals

   1 tbsp raw cane sugar 40 kcals

   3/4 tsp salt

   1 tbsp skimmed milk powder 18 kcals

   1 tbsp sunflower oil 124 kcals

   300ml water

For the raisin/seed dispenser

   1 tbsp sunflower seeds 17 kcals

Using a breadmaker with wholewheat "bake raisin" setting, add the dough ingredients in the order given and leave to run the programme.

Per loaf: kcals 1563
Carbs 304 Fat 23 Protein 58g

Per 50g slice: kcals 123
Carbs 24g Fat 2g Protein 5g

Naan Bread

Freshly made Naan bread is really good for mopping up a dhal or curry and is easy to do. I use white flour for this, so that the bread has a really soft texture. This recipe comes from the cookery book that came with my Panasonic breadmaker.

Makes 4 small Naan

   1/2 tsp fast acting yeast 6 kcals

   250g strong white flour 910 kcals

   1 tsp sugar 16 kcals

   1/2 tsp salt

1/2 tsp baking powder 2 kcals

2 tbsp (25g) Greek style yogurt 13 kcals

1 tbsp sunflower oil 120 kcals

100ml water

Make the dough in a breadmaker on the basic dough programme.

Preheat a grill to very hot.

Divide the dough into 4 balls and roll out into oval shapes, about 25cm x 10cm (10" x 4").

Place on greased baking sheets.

Bake under the grill for 2 to 3 minutes on each side, until brown and well puffed.

Per serving (1 Naan): kcals 268
Carbs 50g Fat4g Protein 7g

Thin Crust Wholewheat Ham and Chorizo Pizza

I make my pizza base using wholewheat flour, or sometimes half and half with white flour, in my breadmaker. I make two pizzas from one batch of dough, which gives a lovely thin and crispy base, which can be frozen with or without toppings. This has become something of a Saturday favourite!

Serves 6 (2 pizzas)

For the dough:

1/2 tsp fast action yeast

300g strong wholewheat flour (wholewheat) 1036 kcals

1/2 tsp salt

1/2 tbsp sugar 46 kcals

1 tbsp skimmed milk powder 6 kcals

1 tbsp extra virgin olive oil 120 kcals

210ml water

For the topping:

180g tomato passata 58 kcals

1 medium onion, finely sliced 46 kcals

70g grated Emmental cheese 252 kcals

2 slices lean ham, chopped 92 kcals

100g chorizo, sliced 412 kcals

4 slices rosette (salami), cut in triangles 188 kcals

100g mushrooms, thinly sliced 11 kcals

20 black olives 100 kcals

250g buffalo mozzarella, sliced 678 kcals

a little extra olive oil to grease the baking trays

Using a breadmaker with pizza dough setting, add the ingredients in the order given and leave to run the programme (45 minutes on my machine).

Brush a little olive oil on two baking trays or pizza trays.

Divide the dough in two and roll out on a floured surface to fit the shape of the trays.

Lay the dough on the trays and prick the bottom with a fork.

Leave to rise for 30 minutes or so if you have time, or until you are ready to bake.

Preheat the oven to 220c (fan).

Spread the passata over the base leaving a little dough clear area around the edges.

Then distribute the onion and sprinkle the grated cheese over.

If I am going to freeze one of the pizza bases I usually do it at this point, then proceed with the still-frozen or defrosted pizza at the next step.

Distribute the ham, chorizo, salami and mushrooms and then dot the olives on top.

Add the mozzarella slices, torn into pieces.

Bake at the top of the oven for 15 minutes until the pizza is golden and bubbling.

Per serving: kcals 509
Carbs 46g Fat 26g Protein 25g

Serve with a crisp green salad.

Wholewheat Maneesh ~ Seedy Flatbread

I got inspired to make this after watching Paul Hollywood's "Bread" series on TV. I used the breadmaker to make the dough and after proving, topped it with sesame seeds and dried herbs. It goes perfectly with **Baba Ganoush** (page 31).

Makes 2 breads, serves 4 - 6

For the dough:
> 1/2 tsp fast acting yeast 6 kcals
> 250g strong wholewheat flour 903 kcals
> 1/2 tsp sugar 8 kcals
> 1/2 tsp salt
> 150ml water

For the topping:
> 2 tbsp sesame seeds 103 kcals
> 2 tbsp herbes de Provence 25 kcals
> 1 tsp olive oil 40 kcals

Using a breadmaker with pizza dough setting, add the dough ingredients in the order given and leave to run the programme (45 minutes on my machine).

Turn out the dough onto a greased surface and divide into two.

Roll into circles, transfer to greased non-stick baking sheets and cover with oiled cling film.

Leave to rise for 20 minutes.

Preheat the oven to 220c (fan).

Mix the seeds and herbs with the oil and spread thickly onto the surface of the breads and bake for about 15 minutes until golden brown.

Transfer to a wire rack to cool.

Per serving (4): kcals 271
Carbs 47g Fat 5g Protein 9g

Per serving (6): kcals 181
Carbs 31g Fat 3g Protein 6g

Rosemary Focaccia

This is a real treat to serve warm with **Tian of Vegetables with Mozzarella** (page 77)

Serves 4

For the dough:

    1/2 tsp fast acting yeast

    300g strong unbleached white flour 1083 kcals

    1 tsp salt

    1 tbsp olive oil 120 kcals

    200ml water

For the topping:

    2 tbsp finely chopped rosemary leaves 4 kcals

    Sea salt flakes

    1 tbsp olive oil 120 kcals

    1 tsp water

Using a breadmaker with pizza dough setting, add the ingredients in the order given and leave to run the programme (45 minutes on my machine).

Working on a floured board, knead half the rosemary into the dough.

Turn out onto a lightly floured surface, flatten gently and shape into a rough circle or oval.

Lightly grease and flour a non-stick baking tray and carefully transfer the dough to it and cover again with the cling film.

Leave to prove in a warm place for 30 to 40 minutes, until nearly doubled in size.

Preheat the oven to 180c (fan).

Mix the olive oil with a teaspoonful of water

Push your finger in to make deep indents in the dough and then brush with the oil mixture.

Scatter the remaining rosemary over the top and sprinkle with sea salt flakes.

Bake in the oven for 20 to 25 minutes until golden.

Transfer to a wire rack to cool slightly and serve warm.

Per serving: kcals 332
Carbs 55g Fat 9g Protein 9g

132

Desserts, yes even on fast days! Or maybe especially on fast days. If you're the kind of person who might reach for a chocolate or something sweet after dinner, then having a dessert can satisfy that need and set you up for a gentle cruise through to bedtime.

And of course on the days in between fasts we can enjoy the best of seasonal fruit, dairy and chocolate....

I've had some fun coming up with desserts that are less than 100 calories, but there are also some indulgences here to enjoy at the weekends or with friends and family.

I have used an ice-cream maker for a couple of these recipes - you can make the recipes without if you don't have one, but I haven't tested the process.

Plum and Ginger Filo Baskets

These little baskets made from filo pastry are pretty sensational and can be filled with all kinds of different fruits, hot or cold. Here I spooned in a prepared compote of gingery-flavoured plums.

The trick is to have two different sizes of ramekins, so that you can keep the centre of the basket open while they baking.

Either bake lightly to just get the shape set, then fill with fruit to be baked inside the pastry, or bake until golden brown and fill with ready prepared hot or cold filling.

Per person

> 1/2 sheet filo pastry 41 kcals
>
> 5g unsalted butter 36 kcals
>
> 1/2 piece stem ginger in syrup 53 kcals
>
> 100g red plums 46 kcals

To serve

> **A dusting of icing sugar**

Preheat the oven to 180c (fan).

Halve and stone the plums.

Put in a small pan with the stem ginger and cook gently with a lid on until just softened.

Meanwhile, melt the butter, and brush a little on the inside of a ramekin.

Cut the filo pastry into four squares.

Lay them into the larger ramekin, overlapping each other to form pointed petals.

Brush the bottom and inside of the pastry with the remainder of the melted butter.

Set the smaller ramekin in the middle and put on a baking tray.

You do have to be careful that the pastry doesn't flop over the middle, or it will break as you try and remove the smaller ramekin.

Bake for 10 - 12 minutes, until golden brown.

Remove from the oven and allow to cool slightly, before carefully removing the inner ramekin.

Fill with the plums and serve with a dusting of icing sugar.

Per serving: kcals 176
Carbs 32g Fat 5g Protein 2g

This would be good with a spoonful of Greek yogurt or crème fraiche.

Strawberry and Rhubarb with Meringue Topping

I was so thrilled to discover that you can make something that has the same lusciousness as a lemon meringue pie, but without the pastry. Rhubarb is a wonderful partner with strawberries and has a delightful tartness that contrasts really well with the slightly sweet berries. If you find that rhubarb is available before the strawberries are in season, then you can use a tablespoonful of strawberry jam instead of fresh fruit (12 calories per serving extra).

Serves 4

500g rhubarb, chopped into 3cm lengths 105 kcals

2 tbsp Acacia honey 128 kcals

half an orange 43 kcals

2 eggs, separated 126 kcals

50g caster sugar 194 kcals

100g strawberries, hulled and sliced 34 kcals

Heat the oven to 160°c (fan).

Use a peeler or sharp knife to take the outer skin from half an orange without any of the pith, then slice into fine strips.

Juice the orange. Put the rhubarb in a shallow ovenproof dish with the honey, orange rind and juice. Bake uncovered for 30 to 40 minutes, until the rhubarb is soft, but still holds its shape.

Meanwhile put the strawberries in a small pan and cook gently until the strawberries have softened, about 5 minutes.

Mix the rhubarb and strawberries with the egg yolks and divide between 4 ramekins. Put the ramekins onto a baking sheet and cook in the oven for 10 minutes.

Meanwhile, whisk the egg whites until stiff, then add 25g of sugar and whisk again. Fold in the remaining sugar.

Pile the meringue on top of the ramekins and ensure that the rhubarb is completely covered. Bake for 10 to 15 minutes until golden brown, then serve immediately.

Per serving: kcals 157
Carbs 32g Fat 3g Protein 4g

Baked Amaretti Stuffed Peaches with Greek Yogurt

This is a simple idea that works with white or yellow peaches or nectarines. I have a richer version of this in my first book *"Focus on Flavour"* but here I have opted for a faster method using less fat and sugar and no egg.

Per person

1 peach, halved and stoned 59 kcals 8 0 1

1 soft Amaretti biscuits 36 kcals 4 2 1

1/2 orange, zest and juice 34 kcals 9 0 1

To serve

1 soft Amaretti, crumbled 36 kcals 4 2 1

75g Greek yogurt kcals 88 kcals 4 7 3

Crumble the Amaretti biscuit and mix with some orange zest, then add just enough orange juice to enable the mix to hold together.

Form into two rounds and stuff the peach halves neatly.

Put the peaches in a baking dish to fit quite closely and pour the orange juice around them.

Bake in the oven for about 30 minutes until the peaches are tender.

Serve with the Greek yogurt and crumbled Amaretti and any remaining orange zest.

Per serving: kcals 253
Carbs 29g Fat 11g Protein 7g

Apple and Quince Feuilletés

Here's another fab thing to do with Filo. Quince is not often found for sale, but it can produce abundant fragrant golden pear shaped fruits, which make a marvellous jelly or paste. You might find it as Pate de Coing (French) or Membrillo (Spanish). it goes really well with apples, but if you have some left over, try having it with some strong hard sheep cheese, like Manchego.

Serves 4

> 2 sheets filo pastry 164 kcals
> 100g quince paste 280 kcals
> 2 dessert apples 70 kcals
> 10g unsalted butter 72 kcals

To serve

> 2 tsp honey 38 kcals

Preheat the oven to 180c (fan).

Melt the butter in a small pan.

Peel and core the apples and cut into slices.

Working quickly to avoid the filo drying out (see *Tip), lay the two sheets of filo on top of each other.

Cut in half and double up the layers, then cut into four rectangles.

Lay them on a non-stick baking sheet or one covered with a liner.

Brush with a little melted butter.

Divide the quince paste between the pastries, dotting it all over.

Lay the sliced apple over the top and brush with the remaining melted butter.

Bake in the oven for 12 to 15 minutes until the apples are lightly coloured and tender.

Serve drizzled with a little honey.

Per serving: kcals 156
Carbs 30g Fat 3g Protein 1g

Excellent with **Frozen Honey and Walnut Fromage Blanc**, or with toasted chopped hazelnuts and whipped cream.

> *Tip: Working with Filo. Because it is made without fat, filo pastry can dry out quickly. Keep what you aren't using covered with a sheet of cling film or a damp cloth while working on a single sheet at a time. When you've finished with what you need, wrap any remaining pastry in cling film and store in the fridge.

Frozen Honey and Walnut Fromage Blanc

I was really pleasantly surprised to find that it is possible to make a really enjoyable frozen dessert without all the fuss of making an egg custard or whisking egg whites. This is delicious with **Apple and Quince Feuilletés**. The addition of a little crème fraîche is important for flavour and creaminess. I used an ice cream maker for this recipe.

Serves 6

> 350g low fat fromage blanc 161 kcals
> 150g crème fraiche 321 kcals
> 2 spoonfuls (20g) acacia honey 54 kcals

25g walnut pieces, toasted 155 kcals

Mix the honey with the fromage blanc and crème fraîche then pour into the ice cream maker.

Add the chopped walnuts after the mix has started to thicken.

I usually transfer to a plastic container and put in the deep freeze for about 30 minutes, then remove 10 minutes before serving - I find that it goes very solid if you leave it for too long and is a much better texture when recently made.

Per serving: kcals 115
Carbs 6g Fat 8g Protein 7g

Chopped ginger makes a nice alternative to walnuts and hazelnuts would be equally good.

Apple, Blackberry and Ginger Crumble

Making individual portions for dessert makes sure that you aren't tempted to have another spoonful - plus it looks so much more elegant. The only sweetness here comes from the ginger and the natural sweetness of the fruit. Using just oats for the topping makes this a wheat-free dessert.

Per person

    1 small Gala apple, peeled, cored and sliced 52 kcals

    3g crystallised ginger, finely chopped 10 kcals

    6 blackberries 10 kcals

    1 tbsp water

    10g porridge oats 6 kcals

    2.5g unsalted butter 19 kcals

Preheat the oven to 160c (fan).

Put the fruit into a ramekin and add a spoonful of water.

Rub the butter into the oats to make a rough crumble and press down on top of the fruit.

Bake in the oven for about 30 minutes, until golden on top.

Per serving: kcals 100
Carbs 20g Fat 2g Protein 0g

You can sprinkle chopped nuts or seeds to the topping for added flavour, crunch and goodness.

Serve with a spoonful of ice cream, Greek yogurt or fromage frais.

Figs Baked with Honey and Crème Fraîche

The fig season for us is short but sweet! So here is a simple but delicious way to use them

Serves 2

    3 fresh figs 152 kcals

    2 tbsp sweet dessert wine (Monbazillac or Muscat de Beaumes de Venise) 24 kcals

    2 tbsp crème fraîche 51 kcals

    2 tsp clear honey 43 kcals

Preheat the oven to 220c (fan).

Cut the figs in half.

Pour the wine into an ovenproof dish and place the figs in it close together.

Put a teaspoonful of crème fraiche on each half and drizzle the honey over the top.

Bake high up in the oven for 5 minutes and serve immediately.

Per serving: kcals 130
Carbs 25g Fat 3g Protein 1g

Rhubarb-Orange-Honey Compote with Cardamom Custard

I used my beautiful home grown forced rhubarb, which I baked with orange juice and zest and a little honey. Surrounded with a delicate, lightly sweetened soya custard aromatised with cardamom and vanilla.

Serves 4

> **500g rhubarb, chopped into 3cm lengths 105 kcals**
>
> **2 tbsp Acacia honey 120 kcals**
>
> **half an orange 43 kcals**

For the custard

> **20g plain flour 70 kcal**
>
> **20g light brown sugar 76 kcal**
>
> **2 large egg yolk 108 kcal**
>
> **500ml natural soya milk 163 kcals**
>
> **3 cardamom pods, crushed**

For decoration

> **1 cup strawberries, hulled and halved 49 kcals**

Heat the oven to 160°c (fan).

Use a peeler or sharp knife to take the zest (outer skin) from half an orange without any of the pith, then slice into fine strips.

Juice the orange.

Put the rhubarb in a shallow ovenproof dish with the honey, orange rind and juice.

Bake uncovered for 30 to 40 minutes, until the rhubarb is soft, but still holds its shape.

Meanwhile, put the cardamom pods and milk into a saucepan and bring just to the boil.

Remove from the heat and leave to infuse for 10 minutes, then strain.

Put the flour and sugar into a bowl or jug and add a little of the milk to make a smooth paste.

Add the rest of the milk gradually, stirring well after each addition to keep the sauce as smooth as possible.

Return to a clean pan and cook over medium heat, stirring continuously with a wooden spoon, until the custard is starting to thicken, but do not allow it to boil.

Pour the custard into individual dessert bowls and put a spoonful of rhubarb in the centre.

Decorate with the strawberries.

Per serving: kcals 191
Carbs 31g Fat 5g Protein 8g

Pear with Chocolate Meringue Topping

Soft sharp pear contrasts wonderfully with a sweet, nutty chocolate meringue topping.

The idea for this dish came from BBC Good Food, but their recipe had way too much sugar for my taste, so I radically changed it. If you want to have a little dessert on a fast day, then make 4 mini ramekins instead - that hit of dark chocolate can make a really satisfying end to your meal for under 100 calories.

Serves 2

> **1 egg white 16 kcals**
>
> **Juice of 1 lemon 12 kcals**
>
> **15g (1 level tbsp) soft brown sugar 45 kcals**
>
> **5g (1 level tbsp) unsweetened cocoa powder, sifted 11 kcals**
>
> **20g (2 level tbsp) ground almonds 115 kcals**
>
> **2 small pears 180 kcals**

Heat the oven to 160c (fan).

Peel the pears, discard the cores and cut into pieces.

Put into a small saucepan with the lemon juice, cover and cook gently for about 10 minutes, until the pear is nice and soft.

Meanwhile, mix the cocoa, sugar and almonds in a bowl.

Whisk the egg white until it hold soft peaks, then gently fold in to the dry ingredients.

Transfer the pears to 2 ramekins and spread the meringue mixture over the top.

Bake for about 20 - 25 minutes, until nicely crisped on top.

Per serving: kcals 180
Carbs 33g Fat 6g Protein 5g

Skinny Tiramisu

This recipe has evolved from an idea by Ainsley Harriot. For the chocolate topping I use a block of 100% cocoa, which is fabulously intense and give loads of flavour for few calories. Amaretti are made with almond flour, egg white and sugar, so they are wheat-free. They provide sweetness and a lovely texture at the bottom of the glass - give an added kick with a hit of coffee liqueur if you have the calories to spare....

Serves 1

2 small Amaretti biscuits 32 kcals

some strong brewed coffee

80g low fat fromage blanc (or fromage frais) 44 kcals

1/4 tsp pure vanilla extract 3 kcals

a handful of soft fruit (strawberries, raspberries, blueberries) 33 kcals

pinch of ground cinnamon 1 kcal

1 heaped tsp grated 100% chocolate 12 kcals

To garnish

A couple of berries, whole or sliced 8 kcals

Optional:

2 tsp Tia Maria, Kahlua or coffee liqueur 30 kcals

2 Amaretti biscuits, for garnish 32 kcals

Put the fruit in a small pan with the cinnamon and a splash of water and cook gently for a couple of minutes until the juice starts to run.

Lightly whisk the fromage blanc together with the vanilla extract to make it light and fluffy.

Put the biscuits in the bottom of a dessert glass and add the liqueur, if using. Pour in enough coffee to just cover the biscuits and let them soften.

Top with most of the fruit and then the fromage blanc. Drizzle the remaining fruit on the top and sprinkle thickly with grated chocolate.

Chill before serving.

Top with some sliced or whole berries or another Amaretti cookie or two, depending on whether it is a fast day or not!

Per serving: kcals 131
Carbs 22g Fat 1g Protein 7g

Cinnamon and Citrus Pineapple

Here's another adaptation of a recipe from the BBC Good Food website, where they have a great variety of low calorie dishes. The addition of cinnamon helps to give a lovely spicy sweetness to it. Buy your pineapples when they are in their peak season in their country of origin.

Serves 4

- 1 medium pineapple 338 kcals
- 10g unsalted butter 72 kcals
- 120g 0% fat fromage blanc (or fromage frais) 56 kcals
- 1 lime 20 kcals
- 2 tsp acacia honey 40 kcals
- 1 tsp ground cinnamon 6 kcals
- 1/2 tsp freshly grated nutmeg 6 kcals

To garnish

- A pinch of ground cinnamon
- Lime zest

Cut the top and bottom off the pineapple, stand on a board and cut away the skin.

Cut in half lengthwise and then cut each half into 4, making 8 even-sized spears.

Cut off and discard the central core from each spear.

Grate the lime zest, or remove the outer coloured layer with a peeler (avoiding the pith) and then cut into shreds, or use a zester.

Cut the lime in half and squeeze the juice.

Mix half of the cinnamon in with the fromage blanc, which you can whisk lightly to create more volume (this doesn't work so well with fromage frais).

Mix 2 teaspoons of honey with the remaining cinnamon and grated nutmeg into the lime juice.

Melt the butter in a non-stick pan and fry the pineapple over medium heat for about 8 minutes, turning so that it is just starting to brown lightly on all sides.

Pour in the lime sauce and let it bubble for a couple of minutes, spooning it over the pineapple to give a good glazed coating.

Serve the pineapple with any remaining pan juices drizzled over and a helping of fromage frais, garnished with lime zest and a sprinkle of cinnamon.

Per serving kcals 135
Carbs 28g Fat 2g Protein 3g

Vary this by adding some finely chopped crystallised ginger in with the fromage blanc - only 31kcal for 10g.

**Do use cinnamon from Sri Lanka (Ceylon) if possible and try to avoid inferior varieties, which are usually Cinnamomum cassia from China or Indonesia, rather than Cinnamomum verum, which is considered safer to use in large quantities. Either variety may be helpful for stabilising blood sugar and lowering cholesterol.

Cherry and Choc Chip Gelato

A light but luscious frozen fromage frais dessert, with cherries, dark chocolate and a hint of kirsch, this is my version of Ben & Jerry's Cherry Garcia – fabulous flavour and not too bad on the calories.

Please note this recipe contains raw egg. I have used an ice-cream maker for this recipe.

Serves 6 (based on 2 scoops per person)

- 50g dark chocolate 52% cocoa 276 kcals
- 100g dark red cherries 63 kcals
- 15ml kirsch liqueur 38 kcals
- 2 eggs 147 kcals
- 50g soft brown sugar 188 kcals
- 500g fromage frais 435 kcals

Pre-chill the ice-cream maker.

Halve the cherries and put in a bowl with the kirsch, then refrigerate until needed.

Chop the chocolate, then refrigerate.

Whisk the eggs until light and fluffy. Add the sugar and fromage frais and mix with the whisk.

Pour into the ice cream maker.

Shortly before the ice cream is ready, add the cherries and chocolate and leave to mix for a couple of minutes longer.

Transfer to a plastic container with lid and put in the freezer to firm up, for up to about 30 minutes, then serve.

Best made shortly before serving.

If freezing for a longer time, remove from the freezer about 30 minutes before serving so that it can soften enough to scoop.

Per serving: kcals 118
Carbs 15g Fat 5g Protein 3g

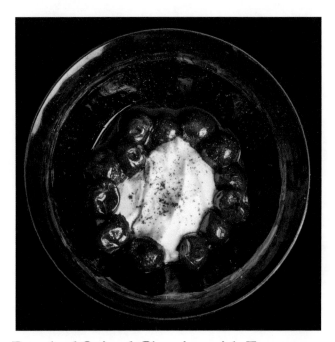

Poached Spiced Cherries with Fromage Frais

This is a quick and easy dessert. When cherries are in season, I stone them and freeze them. Note that no sugar is added, the cherries are quite sweet in themselves and the spice gives the whole dish a bit of a lift.

Serves 1

12 sweet red cherries, stoned 53 kcals
A pinch of mixed spice or cinnamon
100ml water
100g pot 0% fat natural fromage frais 47 kcals

To garnish

A pinch of cinnamon or mixed spice

Put the cherries in a saucepan, with a pinch of 5-spice powder and about 100ml of water. Cook gently, shaking occasionally, until nicely warmed through.

Serve with a little pot of plain 0% fat fromage frais and sprinkle with cinnamon or mixed spice.

Per serving: kcals 100
Carbs 16g Fat 0g Protein 8g

A few toasted flaked almonds on top would be a good addition.

Fromage Blanc with Ginger

This is one of our favourite desserts on a fast day and is a variation of the South Beach diet's Ricotta Crème. I no longer add any artificial sweetener and prefer to use a little stem or crystallised ginger, or some honey or maple syrup, if extra sweetness is needed. If you can't get fromage blanc then use Greek style yogurt, fromage frais, quark or ricotta instead.

Per person

100g 3% fromage blanc 70 kcals
4.5g crystallised ginger 14 kcals

So simple! Just snip the ginger on top and serve. Add a sprinkle of cinnamon perhaps?

Per serving: kcals 84
Carbs 7g Fat 3g Protein 6g

Mojito Cheesecake

Enjoy the wonderful Mexican combination of lime, rum and mint in this simple cheesecake-like dessert.

Serves 4

- 20g unsalted butter 144 kcals
- 40g Amaretti biscuits 192 kcals
- 1 lime 20 kcals
- 250g mascarpone 435 kcals
- 75g St Moret low fat cream cheese 173 kcals
- 20g agave nectar 57 kcals
- 100g 3% fromage blanc 47 kcals
- A handful of mint leaves 4 kcals
- 45ml white rum 98 kcals

To garnish

- 4 thin slices of lime, cut in half
- 4 sprigs of mint
- 4 edible flowers

Melt the butter in a pan and then stir in the crumbled Amaretti, mixing well.

Divide between 4 glasses, pressing down well and making the top even, then chill.

Mix the lime juice, rum and chopped mint together with the agave nectar and leave for the flavours to infuse.

Whizz the mascarpone and cream cheese together in a food processor or whisk until smooth.

Strain the lime syrup and beat in with the cheese.

Spoon over the biscuit bases and chill for at least an hour.

To serve, pipe a little whipped cream onto the top of each cheesecake and top with slices of lime, mint leaves and a flower.

Per serving: kcals 293
Carbs 17g Fat 17g Protein 12g

Raymond Blanc's Chocolate Mousse

I included this recipe in my first book *"Focus on Flavour"* but it is worth repeating here, because for a chocolate mousse it is really quite light and it is absolutely yummy. It is the kind of dessert that I will serve on the last night of one of our photography courses as it makes a great finish! Strangely, although I have served it many times, we have never taken a photograph of it!

Serves 6

- 175g dark 70% chocolate, chopped 950 kcals
- 25g unsweetened cocoa powder 63 kcals
- 7 large egg whites 140 kcals
- 25g light brown sugar 90 kcals
- 1 large egg yolk 55 kcals

Put the chocolate and cocoa powder in a large bowl and melt over a pan of hot water on a low heat.

Stir until smooth, then remove from heat and keep warm over the pan of water.

In another large bowl, whisk the egg whites and sugar until you have soft peaks.

Stir the egg yolk into the chocolate and immediately whisk in a quarter of the egg whites.

Fold in the remaining egg whites with a large spatula, being careful not to over mix.

Pour or spoon into individual glasses and chill for a couple of hours until set.

Per serving: 216 kcals
Carbs 8g Fat 15g Protein 9g

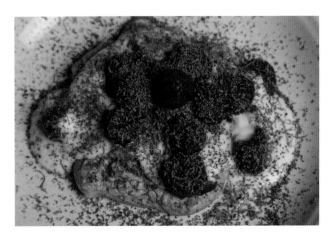

Sticky Meringue with Raspberries and Chocolate

This is based on Nigel Slater's recipe on the BBC Good Food website.

I used 2 egg whites and only 30g golden sugar, making 4 sticky meringues (I don't think you can make a crisp meringue with so little sugar, especially if it is brown). Topped with fromage frais and defrosted raspberries and sprinkled with grated chocolate. Only 75 calories each!!! Yummy! There are things that could be tried for a crisper meringue - use caster sugar instead of light brown, add the sugar slowly, lower the oven temperature and leave the meringue in the oven to dry out after you turn it off. Or just enjoy a slightly sticky and rather sweet indulgence.

Makes 4

    2 egg whites 34 kcals

    30g light brown sugar 113 kcals

    A pinch of cinnamon

    40 raspberries 40 kcals

    1 tbsp 100% grating chocolate 10 kcals

    60g light and thick fromage frais 104kcals

Preheat the oven to 140c (fan).

Spread the sugar out on a baking tray and bake for 30 minutes.

Whisk the egg whites while adding the warm sugar until you have stiff peaks that hold their shape.

Line a baking sheet with baking paper or a non-stick liner.

Spoon the meringue onto the baking sheet into 4 heaps and sprinkle with cinnamon.

Bake for 30 to 35 minutes.

When cooked, flatten the tops to makes indents to hold the raspberries.

Decorate with fromage frais, raspberries and grated chocolate.

Per serving (1 meringue): kcals 75 Carbs 11g Fat 3g Protein 3g

This would be lovely with a sauce made from cherries and kirsch drizzled over the top. Or instead of the raspberries, try slices of banana and slivers of stem ginger and then a little of the ginger syrup drizzled over.

Mini Eclairs with Vanilla Cream

Light and delightful puffs filled with vanilla yogurt, based on a recipe I found in Australian Women's Weekly *"Healthy Heart Cookbook"*. Basically a very light choux pastry, filled with low-fat vanilla flavoured yogurt that has been thickened up using gelatine. Dusted with icing sugar. Less than 50 calories each! (You would probably want to eat at least 2....).

So you really can eat dessert completely guilt-free!

Makes 12

For the eclairs

    5g unsalted butter 36 kcals

    125ml water

    50g self-raising flour, sifted 182 kcals

    2 egg whites 32 kcals

    1 tbsp icing sugar 31 kcals

For the Vanilla Cream

    200g low-fat plain yogurt 142 kcals

    1/2 tsp vanilla essence 6 kcals

    3 tsp light brown sugar 34 kcals

2 leaves gelatine (or 2 pkts powder) 8 kcals

2 tsp water

To serve

a dusting of icing sugar 20 kcals

Heat oven to 180c (fan).

Put the butter and water in a saucepan and bring to the boil.

Add the sifted flour all at once and stir vigorously until smooth.

Transfer to a mixing bowl and leave to cool for a few minutes.

Gradually beat in the egg whites and continue beating until the mixture holds together.

Spoon into a piping bag with a plain 1cm nozzle and pipe lengths of about 5cm onto a non-stick baking tray, making 12 in all.

Bake for 10 minutes, then reduce heat to 160c and cook for a further 15 minutes, until nicely browned.

Allow to cool.

Meanwhile, put the gelatine leaves to soak in a bowl of cold water.

Mix the vanilla essence and sugar with the yogurt in a bowl.

Put 2 teaspoons of boiling water in a small jug and add the drained gelatine, stirring well to dissolve, then pour in to the yogurt.

Mix well, then refrigerate for an hour or so until set.

Just before serving, cut each eclair in half and fill with the vanilla cream.

Dust with icing sugar.

Per serving: kcals 41
Carbs 6g Fat 1g Protein 2g

Serve with fresh mixed berries. Unfilled eclairs may be frozen.

Pear with Amaretti Crumble

Mmm, soft pear topped with a creamy, crunchy topping, and under 130 calories a serving!

There are some lovely European-grown pears to choose from – I used small Williams pears. Similar to my Baked Amaretti-stuffed Peaches and equally delicious, this is a lovely way to end an autumn or winter meal.

Serves 2

2 small ripe pears (about 100g each) 161 kcals

2 tbsp low-fat fromage blanc or fromage frais 14 kcals

2 tsp honey 43 kcals

2 Amaretti biscuits (or other almond biscuits) 32 kcals

Heat oven to 180c (fan).

Cut the pears in half and scoop out the cores with a spoon, leaving a nice smooth hollow, and trim a V shape up to the stalk. Put the pears in an ovenproof dish. Fill the hollows with fromage blanc and drizzle with half the honey.

Bake for 10 minutes, then crumble the biscuits over the top.

Bake for a further 10 minutes.

Serve with the remaining honey drizzled over or around.

Sometimes I add a little water to the dish before baking, which makes a light sauce you can drizzle over (you could use sweet dessert wine for a special occasion).

Per serving: kcals 125
Carbs 30g Fat 1g Protein 2g

Hazelnut and Agave Syrup Baklava

I do like a challenge! I was asked if I could come up with a less syrupy version of baklava and as I had some filo pastry left, I decided to give it a go. I'm pretty pleased with the result: crisp, nutty and slightly sticky Baklava at only 115 calories a slice with a low GI syrup! It was an absolute winner with vanilla ice cream (add 50 kcals per scoop), as it was not as sticky as a traditional baklava.

Makes 8

For the pastries

4 sheets filo pastry 330 kcals

50g ground hazelnuts 324 kcals

1/4 tsp ground cinnamon

20g unsalted butter 143 kcals

For the Syrup

1 tbsp agave syrup 78 kcals

1/2 tbsp orange flower water 0 kcals

3 tbsp water

1/2 tsp vanilla essence

lemon zest, finely sliced

Heat oven to 160c.

Melt the butter in a small pan.

Cut your filo pastry into pieces about 20 x 30cm (8 x 12 inches).

Keep the filo that you aren't using wrapped up in cling film or under a damp cloth.

Take one piece and lay it on the baking sheet, doubled over, so that it is 20 x 15cm.

Brush a little melted butter between the layers and on top (it doesn't need to cover everywhere, just a few light brush strokes).

Repeat with another piece of filo, so that you have 4 layers, lightly buttered.

Spread half the hazelnuts evenly over the pastry and sprinkle with a little cinnamon.

Put another 3 or 4 layers of pastry on, using up any odd pieces, (keeping at least one good looking slice aside) and brushing a little butter on each layer, and on top.

Add another layer of hazelnuts and cinnamon, saving about a half a spoonful of hazelnuts for the top.

Finish with a final 3 or 4 layers filo, lightly buttered and ending with a nice smooth piece on top.

Sprinkle with the remaining hazelnuts.

It's traditional to cut the baklava at this point, into rectangles or triangles, making 8 portions from this quantity.

Bake in the oven for about 50 minutes, turning midway if your oven tends to cook unevenly, until golden brown.

About 10 minutes before the end of cooking, mix your syrup ingredients together in a small saucepan and heat gently.

Remove the baklava from the oven and pour the syrup over.

Per serving: kcals 112
Carbs 10g Fat 8g Protein 2g

Serve warm or at room temperature, with a cup of coffee or maybe a small glass of sweet white wine, like Monbazillac or Muscat de Beaumes de Venise. Really very good with a scoop of vanilla ice cream too (add 50 calories).

Agave syrup is low GI, so better for you in some ways than sugar, and while it is processed, it is not synthetic, though it is high in fructose. It is sweeter than sugar so you need less of it. You could use honey or maple syrup or sugar syrup if you prefer, but you would need to use more for the same sweetness, so the end result would be higher in calories. I didn't add any sweetness to the pastry itself.

Walnuts, almonds, macadamia or unsalted pistachios would work instead of hazelnuts.

I wanted to use rosewater in the syrup, but didn't have any, so I used orange flower water instead. I think the flowery note makes it more middle-eastern, but if you can't get either then use a little lemon juice instead.

I used slivers of lemon zest in the syrup, but orange zest would also be nice.

Plum Kulfi

Kulfi is traditionally made with sweetened condensed milk, which I find rather too sweet. This version is light and fresh and very fruity and makes an excellent dessert after a spicy Indian meal, like the **Baked Haddock Masala** (page 94).

Serves 4

    3 cardamom pods 6 kcals

    300g red plums 138 kcals

    3 tbsp water

    200g 0% fromage blanc 92 kcals

    10g unsalted dry roasted pistachio nuts 13 kcals

Open the cardamom pods to reveal the seeds and then crush the seeds with a pestle and mortar.

Put the plums, cardamom seeds and water in a small pan and cook gently until the plums are really soft.

Set two-thirds of the plums aside and whizz the remainder with a stick blender or in a food processor to a smooth sauce, then transfer to a jug and leave to cool.

Add the fromage blanc to the jug and stir well, then pour into individual moulds and freeze for several hours until firm.

To serve, release from the moulds by dipping each one briefly in hot water, then turn out onto individual serving plates.

Surround with the reserved plums and sprinkle crushed pistachios on top.

Per serving 59 kcals
Carbs 11g Fat 0g Protein 5g

Make this richer and creamier by using 3% fromage blanc. You can substitute fromage frais or ricotta.

Mocha Dessert

This is such an easy and pleasing way to finish a meal. You can use brewed espresso coffee or just mix in some instant espresso granules or coffee essence. I usually use fromage blanc, but fromage frais, Greek yogurt or ricotta would all work just as well. Mix in a little sweetness if you usually drink your coffee sweet, but otherwise there is no need. I use a block of solid 100% cacao chocolate, which is a fantastic ingredient to keep in the fridge for adding to both sweet and savoury dishes.

Per person

    100g 3% fromage blanc 70 kcals

    2 tsp very strong coffee

    - or 1/2 tsp coffee essence

    - or 1/2 sachet of instant espresso granules

    1 tsp grated 100% cacao chocolate 10 kcals

Per serving: kcals 87
Carbs 10g Fat 1g Protein 10g

Lemony Yogurt Cheesecake with an Oatcake Base

Using oats instead of digestive biscuits (Graham crackers) for the crust and delicious Greek yogurt instead of cream cheese for the filling, makes this a much lighter but still delicious alternative to a classic New York Cheesecake.

Serves 8

7 oatcakes, crumbled 408 kcals

50g unsalted butter, melted 359 kcals

70g raw cane sugar 280 kcals

pinch sea salt

1 tsp vanilla extract 6 kcals

600g low fat Greek yogurt 450 kcals

2 large eggs 143 kcals

2 large egg yolks 108 kcals

1 tbsp cornflour 26 kcals

zest and juice of 1 lemon 17 kcals

Preheat oven to 140°C (fan).

Mix oatcake crumbs and melted butter, then turn out into a 20cm (8-inch) loose-bottomed cake tin pan and press mixture into an even crust across the bottom, with the back of a spoon.

Bake for 10-15 minutes until firm and dry, then remove from oven and put on a wire rack.

In a large bowl, beat eggs and egg yolks on low speed, then add sugar, cornflour, salt, vanilla, and yogurt and continue to beat on low speed until light and slightly bubbly.

Add lemon juice and lemon zest and beat briefly to incorporate.

Pour mixture into prepared crust and place in the centre of the oven.

Start checking cheesecake after 50 minutes and then every 5-10 minutes after that, by shaking the pan gently - the filling should look creamy but firm at the edges, and still appear slightly jiggly in the centre (it will firm up as it cools).

Remove from oven and set on a wire rack to cool to room temperature.

Refrigerate for at least 4 hours (or overnight) before serving.

Per serving: kcals 225
Carbs 20g Fat 11g Protein 11g

Serve with **Spiced Lemon Sauce** (56 kcals) and whipped cream (29 kcals) or with **Strawberry Coulis** (34 kcals).

Strawberry Coulis

Perfect to top a simple dessert of fromage blanc or Greek yogurt, to drizzle over ice cream or to top a cheesecake.

Serves 2

>   **100g strawberry pieces 34 kcals**
>   **2 tsp golden granulated sugar 33 kcals**
>   **a few drops of aged balsamic vinegar 1 kcal**

Wash the strawberries and put in a small plan with the sugar and vinegar.

Cook gently for about 5 minutes until soft enough to pass through a sieve.

Per serving: kcals 34
Carbs 8g Fat 0g Protein 0g

Spiced Lemon Sauce

A delicious accompaniment to **Lemony Yogurt Cheesecake** (page 148).

Serves 8

>   **100g raw cane sugar 400 kcals**
>   **2 lemons 34 kcals**
>   **1 tsp ground ginger 6 kcals**
>   **1 tsp ground cinnamon 6 kcals**

Pare the rind from one of the lemons and cut into thin shreds.

Grate the zest of the other lemon. Juice both lemons.

Heat the sugar in a small pan with the juice and stir until dissolved.

Add the spices and half the lemon rind shreds and leave to cool.

When serving, use the remaining lemon rind as garnish.

Per serving: kcals 56
Carbs 14g Fat 0g Protein 0g

Vanilla Custard with Banana

I used soya milk for this but of course you can use dairy milk if you prefer. I do use custard powder sometimes, but when you make your own it becomes quite a grown-up treat as well as being something to share with the whole family.

Serves 2

>   **1 banana 105 kcal**
>   **10g plain flour 35 kcal**
>   **10g light brown sugar 30 kcal**
>   **1 large egg yolk 55 kcal**
>   **250ml natural soya milk 93 kcals**
>   **1/2 vanilla pod**

Cut the vanilla pod in half lengthwise and scrape out the seeds. Put the vanilla pod, seeds and milk into a saucepan and bring just to the boil. Remove from the heat and leave to infuse for 10 minutes, then remove the vanilla pod (you can rinse and dry it and then store it in a jar of sugar to add aroma).

Put the flour and sugar into a bowl or jug and add a little of the milk to make a smooth paste.

Add the rest of the milk gradually, stirring well after each addition to keep the sauce as smooth as possible. Return to a clean pan and cook over medium heat, stirring continuously with a wooden spoon, until the custard is starting to thicken, but do not allow it to boil.

Chop the banana into two bowls and pour the custard over the top.

Per serving: kcals 160
Carbs 17g Fat 5g Protein 9g

Blood Orange with Pistachios

I love the vibrant colour of these blood oranges, but of course ordinary ones would be lovely prepared like this too.

Per person

    1 large orange 86 kcals

    3 dates, pitted and roughly chopped 70 kcals

    6 unsalted pistachio nuts, roughly chopped and toasted 33 kcals

    a sprinkle of cinnamon

Cut the rind and pith off the orange and then slice thinly.

Arrange on a plate and distribute the dates over the top.

Chill until ready to serve.

To serve, sprinkle with cinnamon and scatter the pistachios over the top.

Per serving: kcals 193
Carbs 43g Fat 3g Protein 4g

Banana Ice Cream

This is another recipe that has become very popular with those looking for healthy alternatives to processed and packaged foods. It has a fantastic creamy texture and is not as strongly banana-flavoured as you might imagine. When you have a banana that is perhaps a little to ripe, this is an ideal solution.

Serves 1

    1 banana, peeled and sliced

Lay the banana onto a non-stick tray and open freeze.

Once frozen, transfer the pieces to a Ziploc bag or plastic container and pop back into the freezer.

Remove from freezer about 10 minutes before needed, then blend until smooth.

Serve.

You can add flavourings such as coffee, chocolate, ginger or cinnamon.

Per serving: kcals 105
Carbs 27g Fat 0g Protein 1g

Drinks

We need to drink plenty of fluid on fast days, to keep well hydrated and if possible avoid anything with calories until we are ready to break our fast. So that means finding alternatives to tea with milk, or a cappuccino or coffee with milk or creamer and especially saying no sugar if you are someone who likes their drinks a little sweet.

Even on non-fast days, it is good to have some ideas for refreshing beverages that have little or no alcohol.

So here are some ideas for drinks that you can create yourself to add interest to your water.

I gathered these flowers from a Linden tree and laid them out to dry in the shade for a few days.
A handful in a teapot, topped up with boiling water and left to brew for a few minutes makes a light and fragrant drink.

Herb or Spice Teas

As alternatives to black tea and coffee, explore the world of herbs and spices.

You may just find that you have ingredients growing in your garden, or you can use fresh herbs from the greengrocer - camomile, linden flowers, rose hips, mint leaves, lemon verbena all make delicious light, fragrant and refreshing teas.

You can use slices of ginger, slices of citrus fruit and spices like cloves and cinnamon sticks to make some really delicious and warming hot drinks too.

Pour boiling water over and leave the herbs or spices to infuse for several minutes. Serve in strong glasses so that you can enjoy the attractive colours.

Calories will be negligible and they can help you to appreciate unsweetened drinks.

Many herbs of course have particular properties, for example camomile can be helpful before bedtime, as it tends to have a calming effect, so it is well worth finding out more about those that you enjoy

Sassy Water

We need to drink plenty of fluids on fast days particularly, so if plain water loses its appeal, or you are looking for something different that is cool and refreshing on a hot day, try this.

Some cucumber peel, slices of lemon and orange (or grapefruit or lime), some sprigs of mint and optional borage flowers added to a jug of water (still or fizzy) makes a fantastic refreshing drink for a summer fast day. Keep topping up the jug with more water as needed. Picture overleaf.

Cranberry Fizz

When we had a month without alcohol it was nice to have something different in the evening to relax with. A small amount of cranberry juice (with sugar, not with artificial sweeteners) in a glass, topped up with sparkling water makes a very enjoyable and refreshing cocktail.

Turmeric and Lemon Juice

First thing in the morning, try this:

1/2 a lemon, squeezed into a mug of hot water with a pinch of ground ginger and 1 tsp of turmeric.

This will kick-start your digestive system, so probably best saved for a non-fast day, unless you are planning to eat breakfast.

Vegetable Bouillon

Another thing that can happen on a fast day is that when you drink a lot of water, your electrolytes can get out of balance. It helps to have a salty drink, so try putting a spoonful of Marigold swiss vegetable bouillon powder in a mug and topping up with hot water. It makes a comforting, warming, savoury drink for only 10 to 12 calories, ideal to see you through a dip mid-afternoon. Some people like to use a stock cube, or Bovril or Marmite in the same way.

Grape Juice Spritzer

Here's another non-alcoholic alternative to a glass of wine. I do generally find all fruit juices rather sweet to taste, compared with wine, but they certainly make water more interesting if you are trying to avoid alcohol.

50ml grape juice 32 kcals
250ml sparkling water

White Wine Spritzer

Quite a number of people following the 5:2 way of eating have remarked that they now have a reduced tolerance for alcohol. I have certainly noticed that it goes to my head more quickly! So now if we are going to have a glass of wine before dinner, I make mine a spritzer - about 1/4 wine to 3/4 sparkling water. Lower in calories and less likely to lead to a fuzzy feeling the next day...

I find it helpful to use less oil to save calories, not because oil is bad for you - so here are some techniques that can help reduce the amount of oil you use.

Steam-frying: when you are trying to cut back on calories, a useful technique is to steam-fry. You use just a small amount of oil and some water, stock or soya sauce. Keep the heat lower than you would for stir-frying - this also means that you can safely use oil that has a lower smoke point. Pop a lid over the top to allow the vegetables to get the benefit of the steam and keep the moisture in, but regularly take it off to give everything a stir so that it cooks evenly.

To coat vegetables lightly with oil or dressing - put the vegetables in a plastic bag, add the oil or dressing, and shake gently to distribute it evenly.

Use a silicone brush to paint the surface of a baking tray with the minimum amount of oil needed to stop foods from sticking

Use a silicone liner on a baking tray, then you won't need any oil except where you want it for flavour.

When working with filo pastry, brush oil very lightly on half of one sheet, then fold it over to transfer to the other half. Open it out again and then put the next sheet on top, so that then becomes oily as well. Now turn that sheet over, ready for the next layer to be put on top. You have only used one-quarter of what you would have done otherwise!

Particularly when we first started following the 5:2 way of eating, I found it very helpful to plan ahead, deciding on every meal that we would eat over the duration of a week, and then writing the shopping list to go with the plan. This is particularly important for fast days, as there is nothing worse than getting close to the time for your one meal of the day and then finding that you haven't got the right ingredients!

I started writing up my meal plans and posting them to my Focus on Flavour blog, so you can see examples of them at www.focusonflavour.com/meal-plan

When you work through the meals for a whole week, it gives you a chance to plan the use of leftovers and to work in a good variety of ingredients. I try to include sustainably sourced fish a couple of times a week and to have at least one day when we are mostly vegetarian.

One of the ways that I bring new ideas in to our routine is to look at different styles of cuisine and make up menus that reflect the flavours and ingredients from different parts of the world. This encourages trying out new ingredients and different techniques.

Mexican
Guacamole
Turkey Chilli with Red Beans and Chocolate
Mojito Cheesecake

Middle Eastern Meze
Hummus with Wholewheat Pita - Spanakopita - Keftedes
Lemony Lamb Skewers or Tuna Kebabs with Feta Salad
Hazelnut Baklava 146

Italian
Anchovies with Pinenuts and Capers
Leek Risotto with Parmesan Crisps
Baked Amaretti Stuffed Peaches with Greek Yogurt

Spanish
Gazpacho
Chicken with Saffron and Garlic, Patatas Bravas, Cabbage and Caraway Salad
Apple and Quince Feuilletes

Moroccan
Spicy Cauliflower soup -or- Aubergine Dip with Seedy Flatbread
Chicken & Lemon Tagine
Blood Orange with Pistachios

Caribbean
Spicy Butternut Soup
Jerk Chicken, Avocado & Tomato Salad
Cinnamon Spiced Pineapple

French
Goats Cheese Salad with Warm Lardons
Beef and Carrot Casserole, Dauphinoise Potatoes
Raymond Blanc's Chocolate Mousse

British
Smoked Salmon and Scrambled Egg -or- Watercress Soup
Scotch Eggs - or- Upside Down Fish Pie - or- Sole with Caper Dressing
Apple & Blackberry Crumble -or- Strawberry-Rhubarb Meringue

Indian
Poppadums with Cucumber Raita and Tomato and Red Onion Chutney
Masala Baked Haddock -or- Egg and Mung Bean Curry with Spinach, Naan bread, Kachumber Salad
Plum Kulfi

Thai
Tom Yum soup
Chicken Satay with Cucumber Pickle and Beanshoot Salad -or- Spicy Salmon Patties with Pickled Vegetable Ribbons
Coconut lime ice?

American
Light Caesar Salad
Steak and Mushrooms, Light Coleslaw
Lemony Yogurt Cheesecake -or- Cherry
Choc Chip Gelato

Vegan
Carrot & Coriander Soup -or- Mushroom &
Celery Soup
Oaty Chickpea Crumble with Peach and
Pepper Salsa -or- Nut Loaf -or- quinoa
Plum & Ginger Filo Baskets

Veggie
Goats Cheese Toasts with Beetroot and
Spiced Walnuts
Leek and Crunchy Carrot Gratin
Lemon Tart

Fishy
Smoked Salmon and Avocado Rounds -or-
Smoked Mackerel with Horseradish
Dressing
Tuna Marinaded in Ginger and Garlic,
Swiss Chard with Mushrooms and
Beanshoots
Pear with Amaretti Crumble

Light entertainment
Spring Vegetables with Sesame Wafers
Spiced Red Mullet with Coconut-Lime
Sauce and Puy Lentil Salad
Rhubarb Compote with Cardamom Custard

Fast day faves
Simple Vegetable Soup
Salmon Teriyaki -or- Mushroom Stuffed
Chicken
Mocha Fromage Blanc

"*There is a particular happiness in giving
a man whom you like very much,
good food that you have cooked yourself.*"

~ Karen Blixen, *Out of Africa*

Basic Ingredients

Salt

I prefer to use Sea Salt. My favourite is the large crystals of pure white Maldon sea salt from Essex. I use very little in my cooking, but do find that with increased fluid intake on fast days, that it is especially important to include some salt, to avoid getting an electrolyte imbalance, which can lead to headaches.

Sugar and Sugar substitutes

Over the years I have reduced my sugar usage to a minimum, so now I don't worry too much about using a spoonful or two of sugar for a dessert, though often I find that the sweetness of fruit is enough on its own. I usually choose raw cane sugar.

Sometimes I use honey or maple syrup instead. I have also experimented with using Agave Syrup, but it is high in fructose. I don't use Coconut Palm Sugar (because I believe it has a negative ecological impact) and avoid artificial sweeteners.

Fats

Fats are no longer the demons of healthy eating. In fact low-fat products are often sweetened and have all sorts of additives to compensate for the flavour and texture given by fat. Much better to use the real thing in moderation.

It is worthwhile being aware of the smoke point of different oils - refined oils are actually safer to use at high temperatures than extra virgin oils.

Unsalted Butter

I use this in preference to salted butter for baking, sauces and dressing vegetables.

Nut Butters

Delicious for spreading on toast, or can be thinned with water to make a kind of milk or cream. My current favourite is almond butter. I use crunchy peanut butter for some cooking.

Extra Virgin Olive Oil

For salad dressings and most of my cooking

Sunflower Oil

Where a lighter flavour is required.

Canola Oil

I never use canola (rapeseed) oil as I can't stand the smell of the growing plants.

Groundnut Oil

I sometimes use this where I need a higher temperature for frying

Walnut Oil

Has a wonderfully nutty flavour, but it goes rancid easily, so I tend to avoid having it in my store cupboard. I use vinegar aromatised with walnuts instead for salad dressings.

Sesame Oil

An indispensable flavour for oriental and fusion dishes. Just a few drops add a delicious toasted fragrance and flavour.

Coconut Oil

If I lived in the tropics, I would certainly use it, but it is too expensive to consider using on a regular basis for me.

Lard and Dripping

I use duck fat if I have it, it is an excellent fat to use for high temperature cooking such as sautéing potatoes (an occasional treat…).

Dairy

I gave up drinking cow's milk in tea and coffee many years ago, preferring soya milk, but I do use cow's milk in cooking.

I also use quite a lot of plain yogurt and other fermented milk products, like fromage blanc, which is a great standby dessert with a little cooked or fresh fruit added. It is helpful to have a variety of probiotics in your diet, to assist your friendly gut bacteria.

I'm tending more towards using full fat versions as these don't have other additives to make them taste or behave better, although products made from skimmed or semi-skimmed milk, without additional bulking agents or sugars are fine.

I find that soya milk or oat milk can be substituted for any recipe using cow's milk. Yogurt is handy for bulking up and reducing the calorie count of mayonnaise. Some of the other plant milks, like almond or hazelnut are good too, though often they are sweetened with wheat syrup.

Interestingly, whilst there is a huge variety of cheeses in France, there don't seem to be French equivalents to cottage cheese, ricotta or mascarpone..

Natural Fromage Blanc

Available in full fat, half-fat and low-fat versions. If not available, fromage frais, Greek style yogurt, quark or ricotta can be substituted. Unlike yogurt, this is available in large pots here in France. Fromage blanc is different to fromage frais and can be whipped to make it fluffy (apparently!). It is not as tart as yogurt, not as heavy as crème fraîche or sour cream and not as creamy as fromage frais. It can be dressed up in lots of different ways with fruit, spices, grated chocolate, coffee and so on.

Natural Fromage Frais

I use this interchangeably with fromage blanc. There is a slight difference in flavour and texture. Available in large pots and in individual portions.

Greek Style Yogurt

Has a lovely rich creamy and smooth texture. Delicious to eat on its own, or for making dressings and dips.

Natural Yogurt

There is a bewildering array of different types of yogurts in France: full fat, half fat, light, whipped, strained, Greek, drinking... made from cow, sheep or goat milks... all of which are available made in individual pots, rather than in large containers.

I just avoid the ones that have anything other than fermenting agents added. I most often use 'nature' or 'brassé'.

Cabecou Goat's Cheese

In our region they produce small rounds of goat's cheese, known locally as Cabecou, but often also sold under the name of Rocamadour, one of the most visited places in all of France. In the Spring, when the grass is lush and the young kids have been weaned, the cabecou are at their freshest and lightest in flavour. Left to mature the cheese becomes denser and stronger flavoured. Eventually it will become a hard cheese, that can be grated like Parmesan.

Condiments

Harissa

This Tunisian chilli paste is the traditional accompaniment to Cous Cous. Thin to a runny paste with a little sunflower oil.

Tahini

This sesame seed paste is something that I use for dips and dressings. Available in Middle Eastern, health food and larger food stores.

Tamari

This is a wheat free, naturally fermented Soya sauce, available in health food stores and larger supermarkets, which has a better flavour than ordinary Soya sauce.

Marigold Swiss Vegetable Bouillon powder

Indispensable for making soups and very handy as a quick low calorie savoury drink if you find yourself flagging on a fast day. Organic stock cubes are an alternative.

Walnut Vinegar

Vinegar aromatised with walnuts is a common ingredient here in South West France, where walnuts grow happily.

It is a brilliant ingredient; it brings a wonderful nutty aroma to salad dressings and unlike walnut oil, stores for ages without going rancid. If you can't find walnut vinegar, you could replace the olive oil with walnut oil in a dressing, to get that lovely nutty flavour - otherwise use sherry vinegar or white wine vinegar.

English/US/Australian names for foods

Aubergine / Eggplant

Chickpeas / Garbanzos

Chips / French Fries

Coriander Leaf / Cilantro

Cornflour / Corn Starch

Courgette /Zucchini

Crisps / Chips

Filo / Phyllo

Rocket / Arugula

Spring Onions /Scallions

Sweet Pepper / Bell Pepper /Capsicum

Sweet Potato/ Kumara

Conversion Charts

I have only used metric measurements in describing the ingredients.

Spoonfuls are level, unless otherwise indicated, and should be based on standard measuring spoons, 5ml = 1 teaspoon (tsp), 15ml = 1 tablespoon (tbsp), 1 cup = 250ml

Kilojoules / kilocalories

There are 4.1 kilojoules to 1 kilocalorie

Note: These are approximate only.

Oven Temperatures

C	F	Gas Mark	Temp
110°	225°	1/4	very cool
120°	250°	1/2	very cool
140°	275°	1	cool or slow
150°	300°	2	cool or slow
160°	325°	3	warm
180°	350°	4	moderate
190°	375°	5	moderately hot
200°	400°	6	fairly hot
220°	425°	7	hot
230°	450°	8	very hot
240°	475°	9	very hot

Ovens have a tendency to vary in temperature, one from another. I use a fan oven, and find that I cook the majority of dishes at either 180 or 200 degrees C.

You may need to use a higher temperature than indicated if you are using a conventional oven, or a lower temperature if your oven is particularly efficient.

Liquids

Metric	Imperial
15ml	½ fl oz
25ml	1 fl oz
50ml	2 fl oz
75ml	3 fl oz
100ml	3 ½ fl oz
125ml	4 fl oz
150ml	¼ pint
175ml	6 fl oz
200ml	7 fl oz
250ml	8 fl oz
275ml	9 fl oz
300ml	½ pint
325ml	11 fl oz
350ml	12 fl oz
400ml	13 fl oz
450ml	¾ pint
500ml	17 fl oz
600ml	1 pint
1 litre	1 ¾ pints
1.2 litres	2 pints
1.5 litres	2 ½ pints

Weights

Metric	Imperial
5g	¼ oz
10g	½ oz
20g	¾ oz
25g	1oz
50g	2oz
100g	4oz
150g	5oz
175g	6oz
200g	7oz
250g	8oz
275g	9oz
300g	10oz
325g	11oz
375g	12oz
400g	13oz
425g	14oz
475g	15oz
500g	1lb
1kg	2lb
1.5kg	3lb

Kitchen Equipment

I have used the following kitchen equipment in the course of making the recipes in this book. Details of many of these items and where to buy them will be found on my website at http://www.focusonflavour.com/

I have a 5-burner gas hob and an electric double oven with fan (the top oven has a grill element).

I do not normally use a microwave oven.

Electrical Equipment

Blender

Breadmaker

Food processor with grater and slicer blades

Hand (stick) blender with accessories

- masher, mini processor, whisk

Hand Mixer

Ice cream maker

Panini toaster

Toaster

Pots and Pans

Egg poacher

Heavy cast iron casserole pot

Non-stick frying pans, small, medium and large

Omelette pan

Small and large stainless steel saucepans

Stainless steel saucepan with steamer basket

Wok

Bakeware

Baking trays

Cazuelas (Spanish earthenware dishes)

Dariole moulds

Food Rings

Loaf tin

Loose-bottomed cake tin

Quiche dish

Ramekins in two sizes

Roasting tin

Silicone and non-stick liners for baking sheets

Silicone pop tart mould

Utensils

Assorted steel knives

Colander

Crème Brulée torch

Fork

Garlic crusher

Julienne peeler

Ladle

Lemon squeezer

Microplane grater

Multi surface coarse/fine Grater

Nut chopper

Nylon sieves

Parmesan grater

Peeler

Pestle & mortar

Rolling Pin

Salad spinner

Silicone brush

Slotted spoon

Spatula

Zester

Bibliography

I can read cookery books like other people read novels - the ideas lurk in my mind, waiting for a creative moment when I am searching for interesting combinations and flavourful companions for a dish.

Where I am sure of my sources, I have given credit along the way, but I know that sometimes the provenance of a particular recipe is lost in the mists of time. So I would like to acknowledge all the wonderful food writers and bloggers who have shared their passion for food and cooking techniques and who have helped me to build my expertise and knowledge over the years.

For information about 5:2 Intermittent Fasting, please see

The Fast Diet by Dr Michael Mosley and Mimi Spencer

The 5:2 Diet Book by Kate Harrison

These are my main sources of inspiration and information for this collection of recipes:

Cookbook by Ottolenghi

Simple French Cooking by Raymond Blanc

Nature - simple, healthy and good by Alain Ducasse

The kitchen diaries II by Nigel Slater

Tender volumes I and II by Nigel Slater

The Optimum Nutrition Cookbook by Patrick Holford

Far Eastern Odyssey by Rick Stein

India by Rick Stein

Bread by Paul Hollywood

Cooking to Impress without Stress by Annabel Langbein

The Taste Of Thailand By Vatcharin Bhumichitr

Indian Vegetarian Cookery by Jack Santa Maria

Tapas, the little dishes of Spain by Penelope Casas

The Mexican Cookbook by Sue Style

There days I am as likely to turn to the web for recipes as I am to go to my bookshelf and there are sources that I return to time and again when looking for new ideas, which include: -

BBC Good Food www.bbcgoodfood.com

The Guardian Food pages www.theguardian.com/lifeandstyle/food-and-drink

I would also like to suggest a couple of 5:2 blogs: -

Tinned Tomatoes www.tinnedtomatoes.com by Jacqueline Meldrum

Lavender and Lovage www.lavenderandlovage.com by Karen Burns-Booth

Index

Acknowledgements

My thanks go to Graham, who kick-started our 5:2 journey and has joined me in embracing healthy eating as a way of life. He has helped with setting up and executing much of the photography for this book and inspired me to create delicious and tasty meals along the way. Not only that, but he has been a diligent proofreader.

Graham is my primary taster, who has eaten, commented on and enjoyed every recipe, the lucky chap! I would also like to thank all my guinea-pigs, especially Brenda and Arnold Page and Rita and Dave Beasley - whose visits here have so often combined hard work in the garden, followed by the reward of trying out one of my experiments. My more regular guests, Tricia Jewell and Wyn and Paul Galpin can also take credit for tasting and giving the nod to some of my creations.

With enormous respect and thanks to Dr. Michael Mosley for the Horizon documentary "Eat, Fast, Live Longer", thank you for devising a simple and easy to follow way of eating that has changed our lives for the better.

I would also like to acknowledge and thank all my new-found friends on the 5:2 Intermittent Fasting Diet group on Facebook, who have inspired me with their wonderful stories and helped me and countless others to enjoy our fast days and learn more about eating and living in a sustainable way for long term health and fitness.

Printed in Great Britain
by Amazon.co.uk, Ltd.,
Marston Gate.